Sing Hey diddle diddle

**66 nursery rhymes with their traditional tunes
chosen by Beatrice Harrop**

**with piano arrangements by Beatrice Harrop and Brian Hunt
guitar chords by Chris and John Hoggarth
and illustrations by Frank Francis and Bernard Cheese**

A & C Black · London

Contents

First published 1983 by A & C Black (Publishers) Ltd
35 Bedford Row London WC1R 4JH
© 1983 A & C Black (Publishers) Ltd

ISBN 0-7136-2334-9

Printed in Hong Kong by Dai Nippon Printing Co. Ltd

Acknowledgements

The colour illustrations in the text of this book are from *The Great Big Book of Nursery Rhymes*, chosen by Peggy Blakeley and illustrated by Frank Francis.

The piano accompaniments to songs 1–15, 22, 28, 36–38, 40–51 and 64 are by Brian Hunt and the accompaniments to songs 16–21, 23–27, 29–35, 39, 52–63, 65 and 66 are by Beatrice Harrop. Grateful thanks are due to Chris and John Hoggarth for the guitar chords.

The cover design and the black and white illustrations in the text are by Bernard Cheese.

1 Bobby Shafto

Bobby Shafto's gone to sea,
Silver buckles on his knee.
He'll come back and marry me,
Bonny Bobby Shafto.

Bobby Shafto's bright and fair,
Combing down his yellow hair.
He's my love for evermore,
Bonny Bobby Shafto.

Bobby Shafto's gone to sea,
Silver buckles on his knee.
He'll come back and marry me,
Bonny Bobby Shafto.

F (E*)   C (B7)

Bob-by Shaf-to's gone to sea, — Sil-ver buck-les on his knee. —

F (E)   Bb (A)   C (B7)   F (E)   Fine

He'll come back and mar-ry me, — Bon-ny Bob-by Shaf - to.

F (E)   C (B7)

Bob-by Shaf-to's bright and fair, Comb-ing down his yel - low hair.

F (E)   Bb (A)   C (B7)   F (E)   D.C. al Fine

He's my love for ev - er-more, Bon-ny Bob-by Shaf - to.

* capo on first fret may be used with alternative chords in brackets

2 Baa, baa, black sheep

Baa, baa, black sheep,
    Have you any wool?
Yes, sir, yes, sir,
    Three bags full;
One for the master,
    And one for the dame,
And one for the little boy
    Who lives down the lane.

Baa, baa, black sheep, Have you a - ny wool?

Yes, sir, yes, sir, Three bags full;

One for the mas - ter, And one for the dame, And

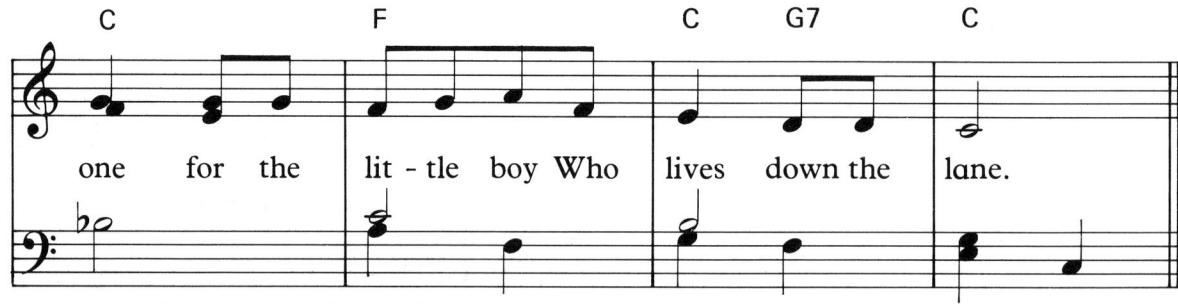

one for the lit - tle boy Who lives down the lane.

3 Cock-a-doodle-doo!

Cock-a-doodle-doo!
My dame has lost her shoe,
My master's lost his fiddling stick
And doesn't know what to do.

Cock-a-doodle-doo!
What is my dame to do?
Till master finds his fiddling stick
She'll dance without her shoe.

Cock-a-doodle-doo!
My dame has found her shoe,
And master's found his fiddling stick,
Sing doodle-doodle-doo.

Cock-a-doodle-doo!
My dame will dance with you,
While master fiddles his fiddling stick
For dame and doodle-doo.

Cock - a - doo - dle - doo! _____ My
dame has lost her shoe, _____ My
mas - ter's lost his fid - dling stick And
does - n't know what to do.

4 Little Tom Tucker

Little Tom Tucker sings for his supper.
What shall we give him?
White bread and butter.
How will he cut it without any knife?
How will he marry without any wife?

Lit-tle Tom Tuck-er sings for his sup-per.

What shall we give ___ him? White bread and but-ter.

How will he cut it with-out a-ny knife?

How will he mar-ry with-out a-ny wife?

5 Jack and Jill

Jack and Jill went up the hill
  To fetch a pail of water;
Jack fell down and broke his crown,
  And Jill came tumbling after.

Up Jack got and home did trot
  As fast as he could caper;
Went to bed to mend his head
  With vinegar and brown paper.

Jill came in, how she did grin
  To see Jack's paper plaster;
Mother, vexed, did whip her next
  For causing Jack's disaster.

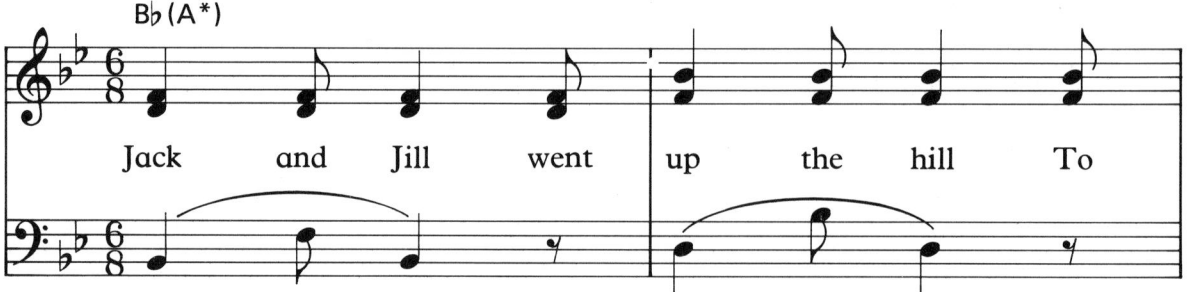

Jack and Jill went up the hill To

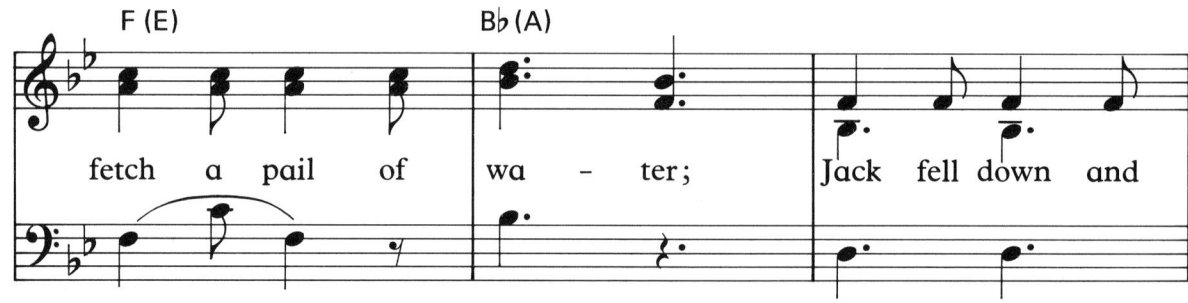

fetch a pail of wa – ter; Jack fell down and

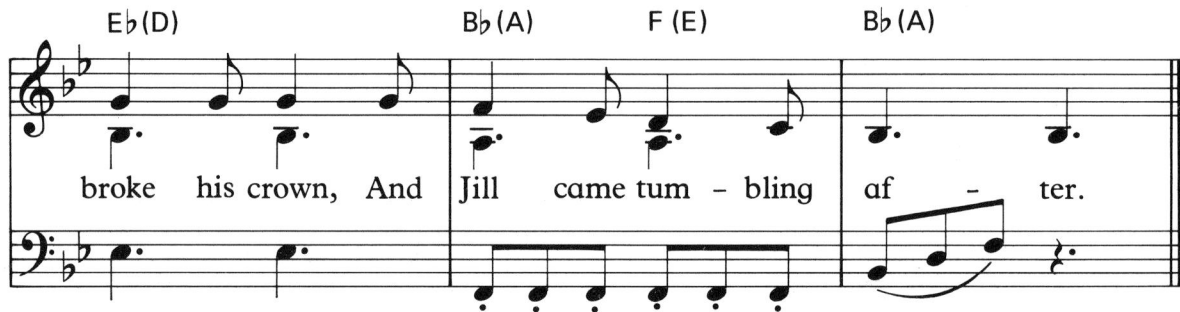

broke his crown, And Jill came tum – bling af – ter.

* capo on first fret may be used with alternative chords in brackets

6 Ding dong bell

Ding dong bell,
Pussy's in the well.

Who put her in?
Little Johnny Green.

Who pulled her out?
Little Tommy Stout.

What a naughty boy was that
To drown poor pussy cat,
Who ne'er did any harm
But killed all the mice
    in his father's barn.

E* B7 E | E B7 E | E B7 E

Ding dong bell, | Pus-sy's in the well. | Who put her in?

E B7 E | E B7 E | A B7 E

Lit-tle John-ny Green. | Who pulled her out? | Lit-tle Tom-my Stout. What a

E B7 E | A B7 E

naugh-ty boy was that To | drown poor pus-sy cat, Who

E B7 E B7 | E B7 E A | E B7 E

ne'er did a-ny harm But | killed __ all the mice in __ his | fa - ther's barn.

* capo on first fret will allow this song to be sung in Key F as written

7 Oh, dear! What can the matter be?

Oh, dear! what can the matter be?
Oh, dear! what can the matter be?
Oh, dear! what can the matter be?
Johnny's so long at the fair.

He promised to buy me a basket
of posies,
A garland of lilies, a garland
of roses.
He promised to buy me a bunch
of blue ribbons
To tie up my bonny brown hair.

Oh, dear! what can the matter be?
Oh, dear! what can the matter be?
Oh, dear! what can the matter be?
Johnny's so long at the fair.

8 Girls and boys come out to play

Girls and boys, come out to play,
The moon doth shine as bright as day.
Leave your supper and leave your sleep,
And join your playfellows in the street.

Come with a whoop and come with a call,
Come with a good will or not at all.
Up the ladder and down the wall,
A half-penny loaf will serve us all.

You find milk and I'll find flour,
And we'll have a pudding in half an hour.

Girls and boys, come out to play,
The moon doth shine as bright as day.
Leave your supper and leave your sleep,
And join your playfellows in the street.

Girls and boys, come out to play, The moon doth shine_ as bright as day. Leave your sup-per and leave your sleep, And join your play-fel-lows in the street. Come with a whoop and

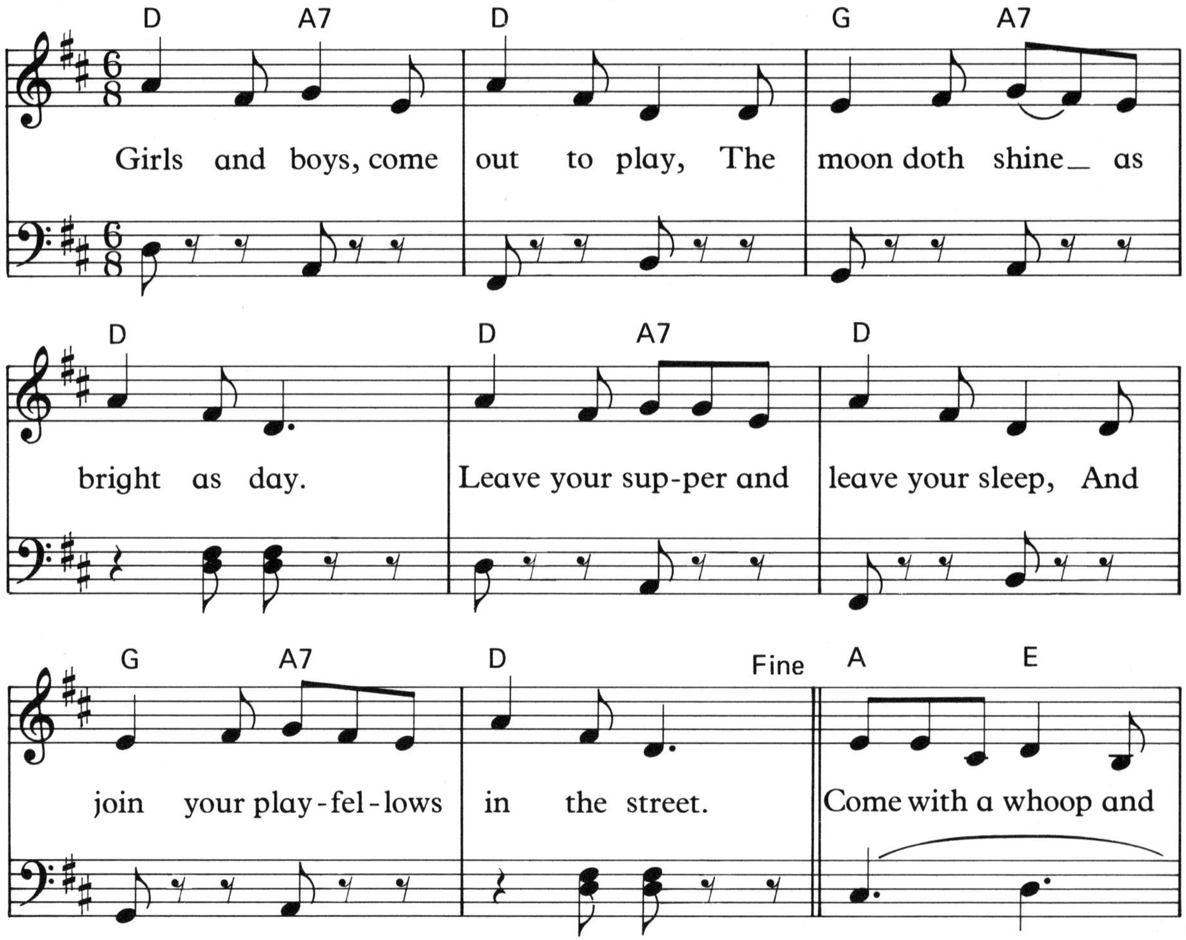

9 Mary had a little lamb

Mary had a little lamb,
    Little lamb, little lamb,
Mary had a little lamb,
    Its fleece was white as snow.

And everywhere that Mary went,
    Mary went, Mary went,
And everywhere that Mary went,
    That lamb was sure to go.

It followed her to school one day,
    School one day, school one day,
It followed her to school one day,
    That was against the rules.

It made the children laugh and play,
    Laugh and play, laugh and play,
It made the children laugh and play,
    To see a lamb at school.

"Why does the lamb love Mary so?
    Mary so? Mary so?
Why does the lamb love Mary so?"
    The eager children cry.

"Why, Mary loves the lamb, you know!
    Lamb, you know! Lamb, you know!
Why, Mary loves the lamb, you know!"
    The teacher did reply.

* capo on first fret may be used with alternative chords in brackets

10 Sing a song of sixpence

Sing a song of sixpence,
A pocket full of rye,
Four and twenty blackbirds
Baked in a pie.
When the pie was opened
The birds began to sing;
Wasn't that a dainty dish
To set before the king?

The king was in his
        counting-house,
Counting out his money,
The queen was in the parlour,
Eating bread and honey,
The maid was in the garden,
Hanging out the clothes,
When down came a blackbird
And pecked off her nose.

They made such a commotion
That little Jenny Wren
Flew down into the garden
And popped it on again.

11 Humpty Dumpty

Humpty Dumpty sat on a wall.
Humpty Dumpty had a great fall.
All the king's horses and all the king's men
Couldn't put Humpty together again.

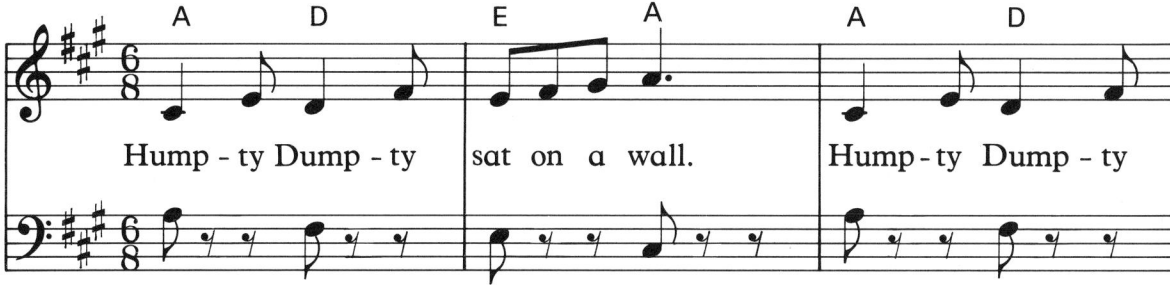

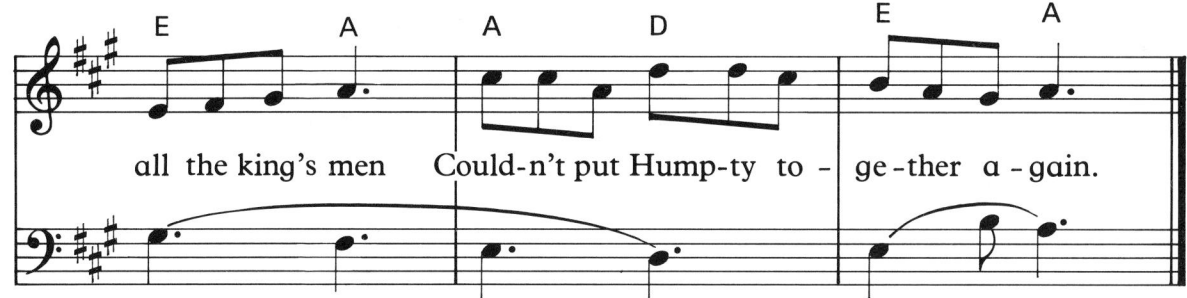

12 The north wind doth blow

The north wind doth blow,
And we shall have snow,
And what will poor robin do then,
    Poor thing?
He'll sit in a barn,
And keep himself warm,
And hide his head under his wing,
    Poor thing!

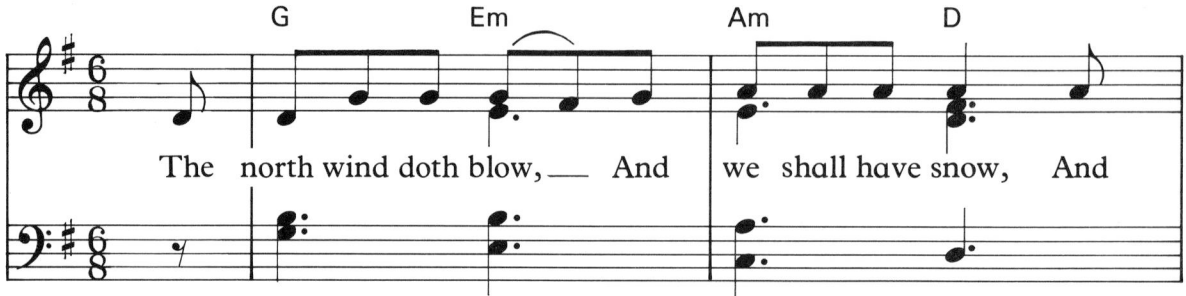

The north wind doth blow, ___ And we shall have snow, And

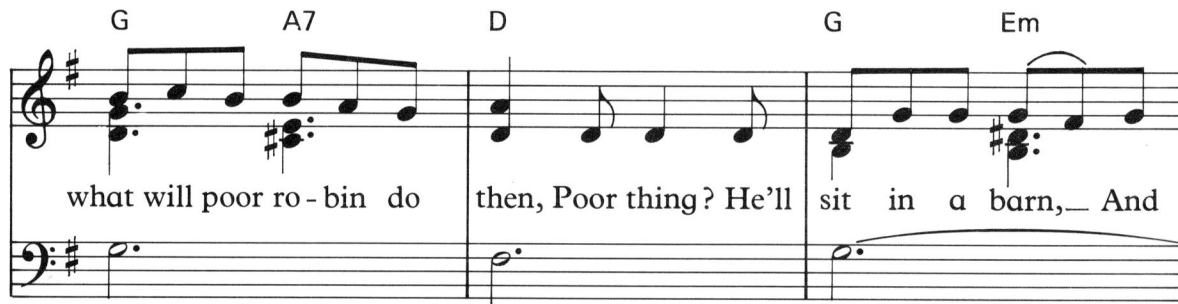

what will poor ro-bin do then, Poor thing? He'll sit in a barn, ___ And

keep him-self warm, And hide his head un-der his wing, Poor thing!

13 Tom, he was a piper's son

Tom, he was a piper's son,
He learnt to play when he was young,
But all the tune that he could play
Was "Over the hills and far away".
Over the hills and a great way off,
The wind will blow my top-knot off.

Tom with his pipe made such a noise,
That he pleased both the girls and boys,
And they all stopped to hear him play,
"Over the hills and far away".
Over the hills and a great way off,
The wind will blow my top-knot off.

Tom played his pipe with such good will
That those who heard him could ne'er keep still;
As soon as he played they began to dance,
E'en pigs on their hind legs began to prance.
Over the hills and a great way off,
The wind will blow my top-knot off.

Dolly was milking her cow one day,
Tom took out his pipe and began to play,
So Doll and the cow danced the "Cheshire Round"
Till the pail was broken and the milk
    ran on the ground.
Over the hills and a great way off,
The wind will blow my top-knot off.

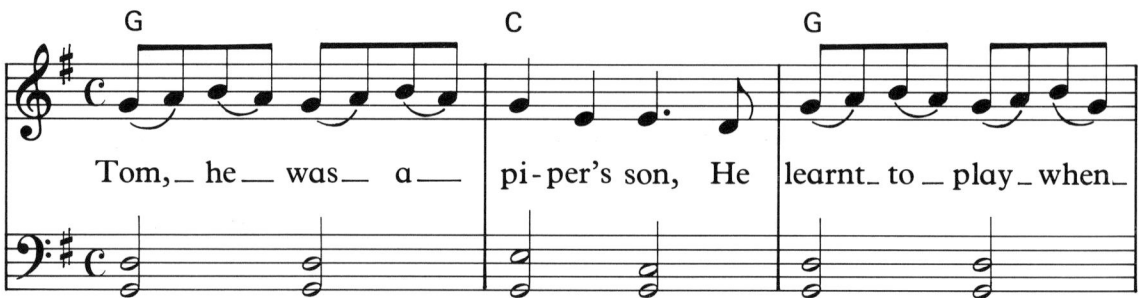

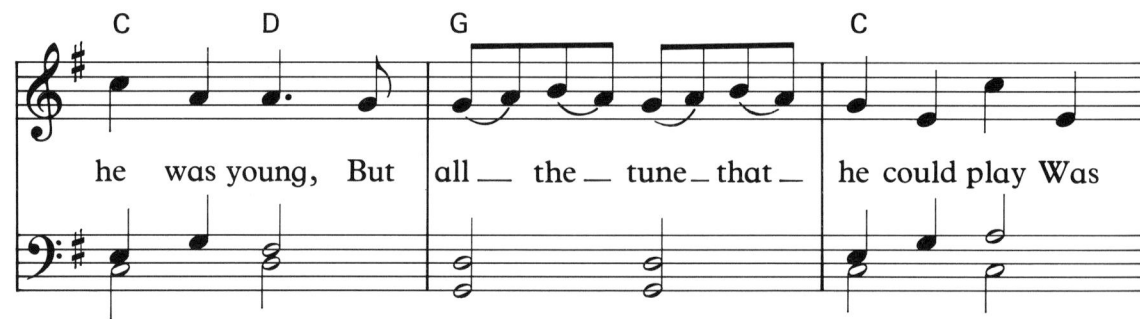

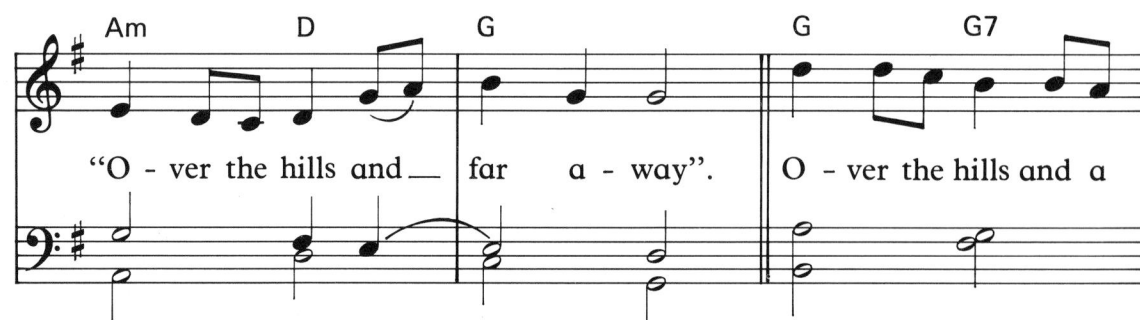

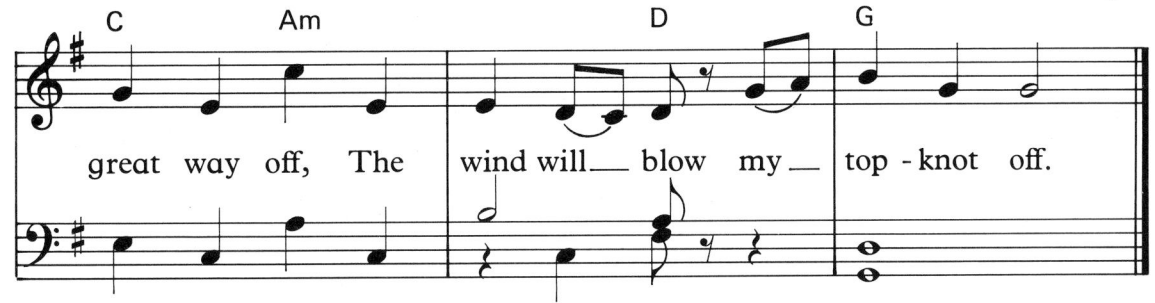

great way off, The wind will_ blow my _ top-knot off.

He met Dame Trot with a basket of eggs,
Tom used his pipe, and she used her legs;
She danced about till her eggs were all broke,
She began to fret, but he laughed at the joke.
Over the hills and a great way off,
The wind will blow my top-knot off.

He saw a cross fellow who was beating an ass,
All laden with pans, pots, dishes and glass;
He took out his pipe and played them a tune,
And the donkey's load was lightened full soon.
Over the hills and a great way off,
The wind will blow my top-knot off.

14 Mary, Mary, quite contrary

Mary, Mary, quite contrary,
How does your garden grow?
With silver bells
And cockle-shells,
And pretty maids all in a row.

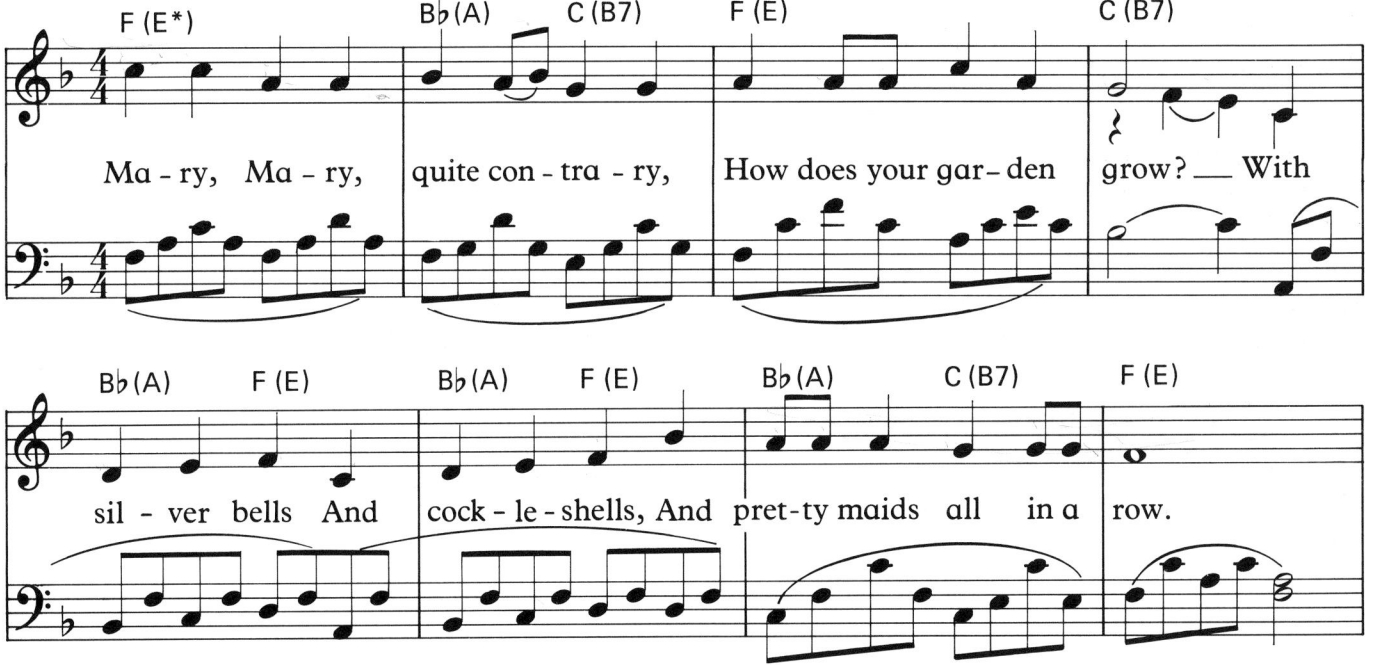

* capo on first fret may be used with alternative chords in brackets

15 Doctor Foster went to Gloucester

Doctor Foster went to Gloucester
In a shower of rain.
He trod in a puddle,
Right up to his middle,
And never went there again.

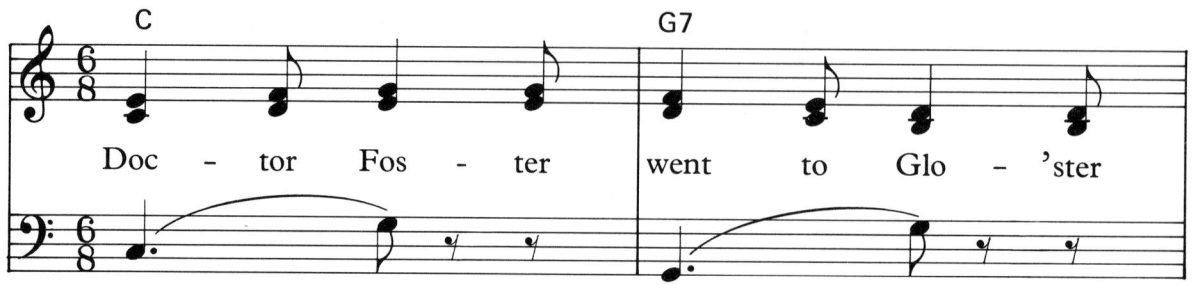

16 Hush-a-bye, baby

Hush-a-bye, baby, on the tree top.
When the wind blows the cradle will rock;
When the bough breaks the cradle will fall,
Down will come baby, cradle, and all.

Rock-a-bye, baby, your cradle is green,
Father's a nobleman, mother's a queen;
Betty's a lady and wears a gold ring;
Johnny's a drummer and drums for the king.

Hush - a - bye, ba - by, on the tree top.

When the wind blows the cra - dle will rock;

When the bough breaks the cra - dle will fall,

Down will come ba - by, cra - dle, and all.

17 I love little pussy

I love little pussy,
    Her coat is so warm,
And if I don't hurt her
    She'll do me no harm.

So I'll not pull her tail,
    Nor drive her away,
But pussy and I
    Very gently will play.

She shall sit by my side
    And I'll give her some food;
And pussy will love me
    Because I am good.

I ___ love lit - tle pus - sy, Her coat is so warm, And ___ if I don't hurt her She'll do me no ___ harm.

18 Lavender's blue

Lav - en - der's blue, did-dle, did-dle, Lav - en - der's green;
When I am king, did-dle, did-dle, You shall be queen.

Lavender's blue, diddle, diddle,
    Lavender's green;
When I am king, diddle, diddle,
    You shall be queen.

Call up your men, diddle, diddle,
    Set them to work;
Some to the plough, diddle, diddle,
    Some to the fork.

Some to make hay, diddle, diddle,
    Some to cut corn;
While you and I, diddle, diddle,
    Keep ourselves warm.

19 Georgie Porgie

Georgie Porgie, pudding and pie,
Kissed the girls and made them cry;
When the boys came out to play,
Georgie Porgie ran away.

20 Three blind mice

Three blind mice,
Three blind mice,
See how they run!
See how they run!
They all ran after the farmer's wife,
Who cut off their tails with a carving knife,
Did ever you see such a thing in your life
As three blind mice?

Three blind mice, Three blind mice, See how they run! See how they run! They all ran after the farm-er's wife, Who cut off their tails with a carv-ing knife, Did ev-er you see such a thing in your life As three blind mice?

21 Pussy cat, pussy cat

Pussy cat, pussy cat, where have you been?
I've been to London to look at the Queen.
Pussy cat, pussy cat, what did you there?
I frightened a little mouse under her chair.

22 There was a crooked man

There was a crooked man,
  And he walked a crooked mile,
He found a crooked sixpence
  Against a crooked stile;
He bought a crooked cat,
  Which caught a crooked mouse,
And they all lived together
  In a little crooked house.

There was a croo-ked man, And he walked a croo-ked mile, He found a croo-ked six-pence A-gainst a croo-ked stile; He bought a croo-ked cat, Which caught a croo-ked mouse, And they all lived to-ge-ther In a lit-tle croo-ked house.

23 The lion and the unicorn

The lion and the unicorn
  Were fighting for the crown;
The lion beat the unicorn
  All round about the town.
Some gave them white bread,
  And some gave them brown;
And some gave them plum cake
  And drummed them out of town.

24 London Bridge is falling down

London Bridge is falling down,
　Falling down, falling down,
London Bridge is falling down,
　My fair lady.

How shall we build it up again,
　Up again, up again,
How shall we build it up again,
　My fair lady?

Build it up with silver and gold . . .

Silver and gold will be stolen away . . .

Build it up with wood and clay . . .

Wood and clay will wash away . . .

Build it up with iron and steel . . .

Iron and steel will bend and bow . . .

Build it up with stone so strong . . .

Stone will last for ages long . . .

25 Tom, Tom, the piper's son

Tom, Tom, the piper's son,
Stole a pig and away did run;
The pig was eat
And Tom was beat,
And Tom went howling down the street.

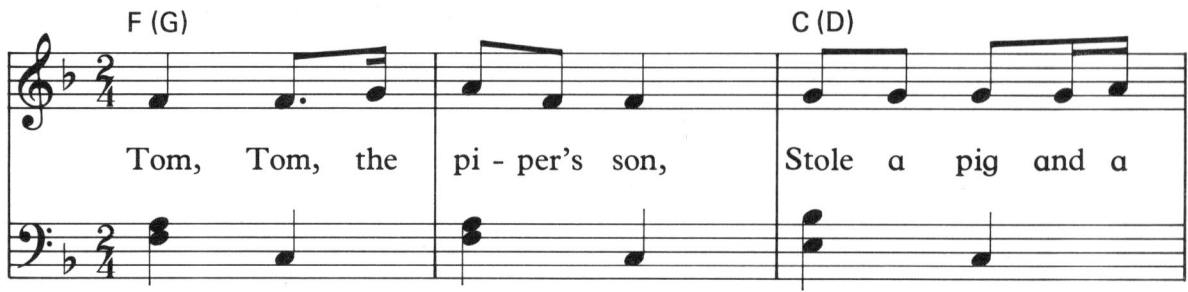

Tom, Tom, the pi-per's son, Stole a pig and a

way did run; The pig was eat And

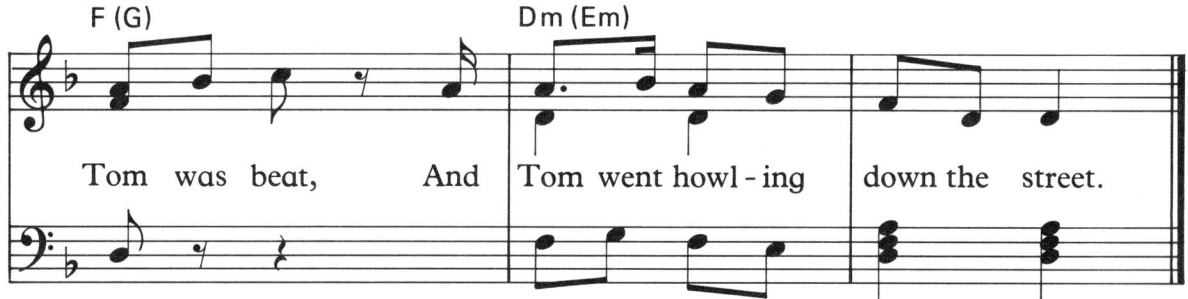

Tom was beat, And Tom went howl-ing down the street.

26 Little Bo-Peep

Little Bo-Peep has lost her sheep
And can't tell where to find them.
Leave them alone, and they'll come home,
Bringing their tails behind them.

Little Bo-Peep fell fast asleep,
And dreamt she heard them bleating;
But when she awoke, she found it a joke,
For they were still a-fleeting.

Then up she took her little crook,
Determined for to find them;
She found them indeed, but it made her heart bleed,
For they'd left their tails behind them.

It happened one day, as Bo-Peep did stray
Into a meadow hard by,
There she espied their tails side by side,
All hung on a tree to dry.

She heaved a sigh, and wiped her eye
And ran over hill and dale, O!
And tried what she could, as a shepherdess should,
To tack to each sheep its tail, O!

*capo on first fret may be used with alternative chords in brackets

27 Little Boy Blue

Little Boy Blue,
  Come blow your horn,
The sheep's in the meadow,
  The cow's in the corn;
But where is the boy
  Who looks after the sheep?
He's under a haycock,
  Fast asleep.
Will you wake him?
  No, not I,
For if I do,
  He'll be sure to cry.

Lit - tle Boy Blue, Come blow ___ your horn, The sheep's in the mea-dow, The cow's in the corn; But where is the boy Who looks af - ter the sheep? He's under a hay - cock, Fast a - sleep. Will ___ you wake him? No, ___ not I, For if I do, He'll be sure ___ to cry.

28 Where are you going to, my pretty maid?

Where are you going to, my pretty maid?
Where are you going to, my pretty maid?
I'm going a-milking, sir, she said,
Sir, she said, sir, she said,
I'm going a-milking, sir, she said.

May I go with you, my pretty maid?
May I go with you, my pretty maid?
You're kindly welcome, sir, she said,
Sir, she said, sir, she said,
You're kindly welcome, sir, she said.

Say, will you marry me, my pretty maid?
Say, will you marry me, my pretty maid?
Yes, if you please, kind sir, she said,
Sir, she said, sir, she said,
Yes, if you please, kind sir, she said.

What is your fortune, my pretty maid?
What is your fortune, my pretty maid?
My face is my fortune, sir, she said,
Sir, she said, sir, she said,
My face is my fortune, sir, she said.

Then I can't marry you, my pretty maid,
Then I can't marry you, my pretty maid.
Nobody asked you, sir, she said,
Sir, she said, sir, she said,
Nobody asked you, sir, she said.

* capo on first fret may be used with alternative chords in brackets

29 Little Jack Horner

Little Jack Horner
Sat in the corner,
Eating his Christmas pie.
He put in his thumb,
And pulled out a plum,
And said, "What a good boy am I!"

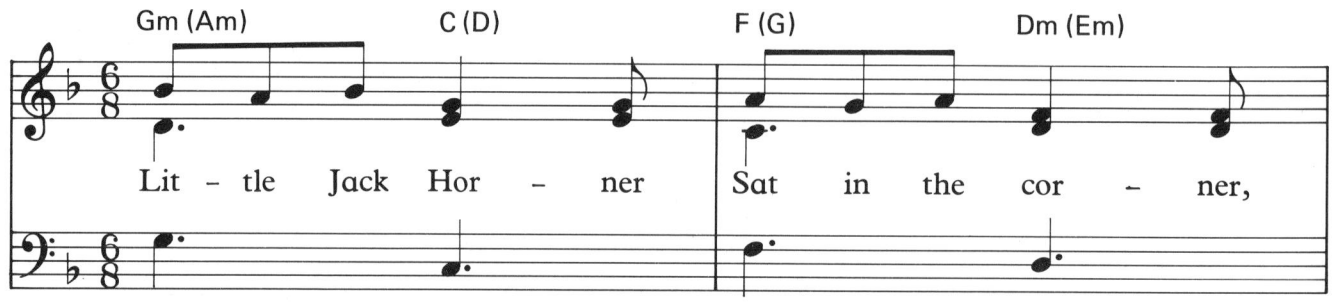

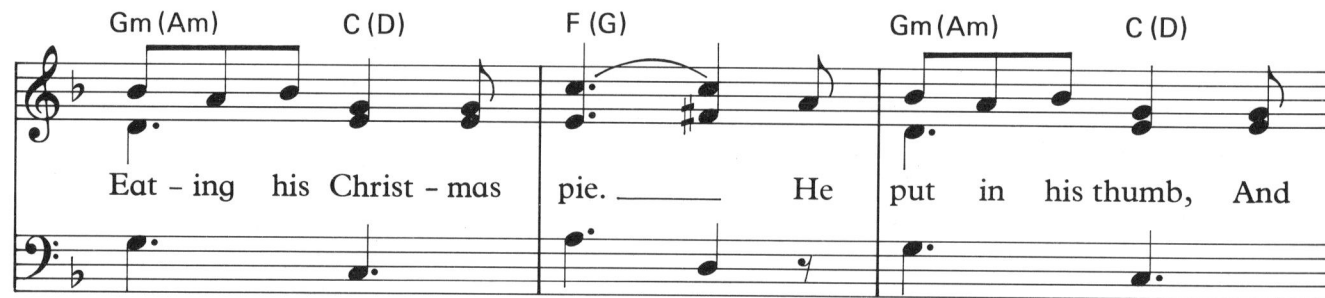

* capo on first fret may be used with alternative chords in brackets

30 Little Miss Muffet

Little Miss Muffet,
She sat on a tuffet,
Eating her curds and whey;
There came a big spider,
Who sat down beside her,
And frightened Miss Muffet away.

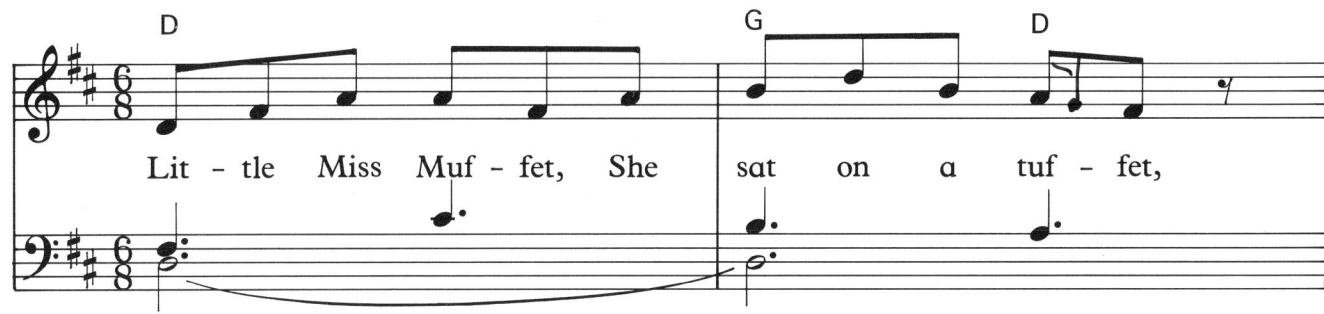

Lit – tle Miss Muf – fet, She sat on a tuf – fet,

Eat – ing her curds ___ and whey; _____ There came a big spi – der, Who

sat down be – side her, And fright – ened Miss Muf – fet a – way. ___

31 Goosey, goosey gander

Goosey, goosey gander,
Whither shall I wander?
Upstairs and downstairs,
And in my lady's chamber.
There I met an old man
Who wouldn't say his prayers,
So I took him by the left leg
And threw him down the stairs.

Goos-ey, goos-ey gan – der, Whi-ther shall I wan – der?

Up – stairs and down – stairs, And in my la – dy's cham – ber.

There I met an old man Who would-n't say his prayers, So I

took him by the left leg And threw him down the stairs.

32 Dance to your daddy

Dance to your daddy,
my little laddie,
Dance to your daddy,
my little man.
You shall have a fishy
on a little dishy.
You shall have a fishy
when the boat comes in.
Dance to your daddy,
my little laddie,
Dance to your daddy,
my little man.

33 Diddle, diddle, dumpling

Diddle, diddle, dumpling, my son John,
Went to bed with his trousers on;
One shoe off, and one shoe on,
Diddle, diddle, dumpling, my son John.

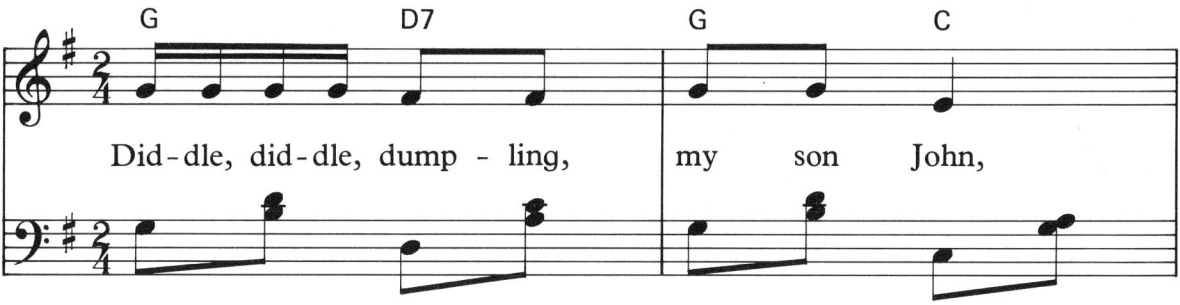

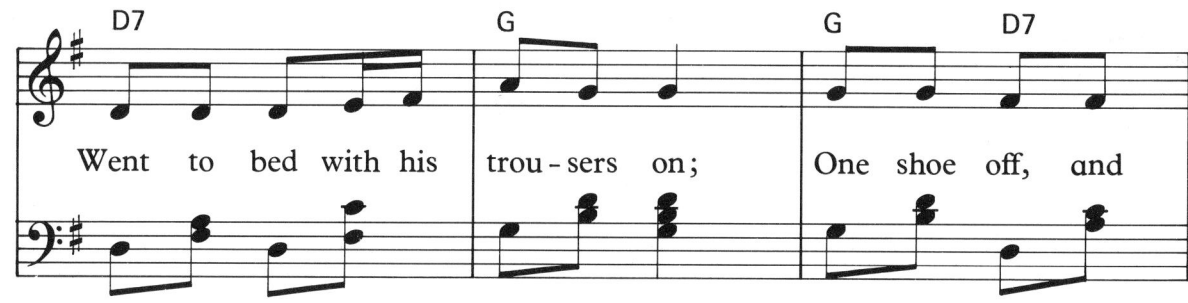

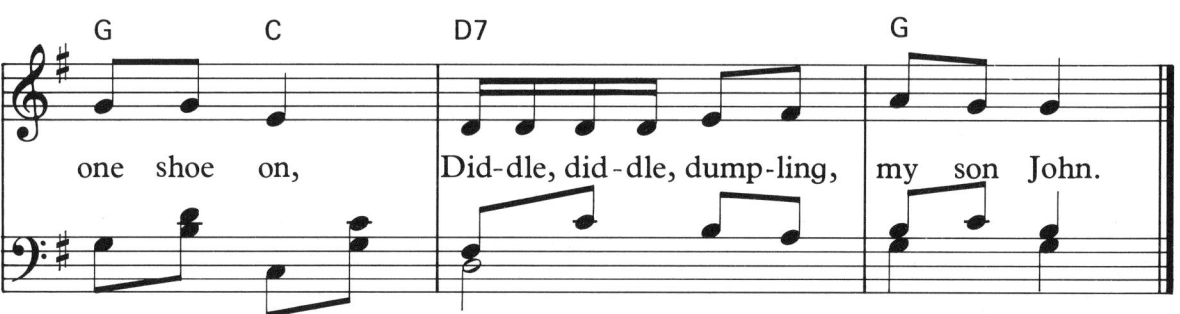

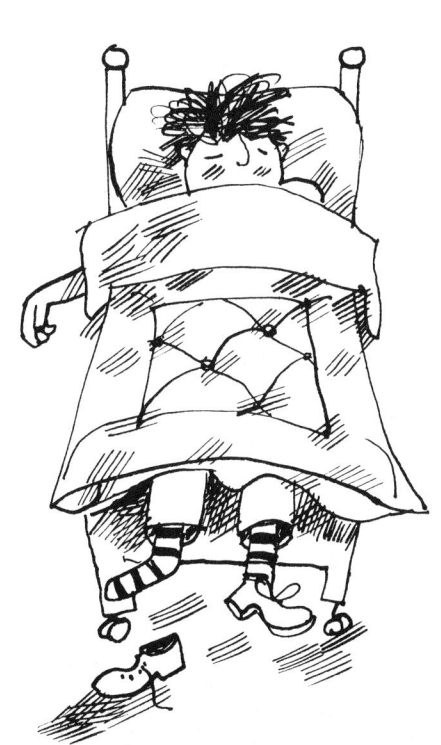

34 One, two, three, four, five

One, two, three, four, five,
Once I caught a fish alive;
Six, seven, eight, nine, ten,
Then I let it go again.
Why did you let it go?
Because it bit my finger so.
Which finger did it bite?
This little finger on the right.

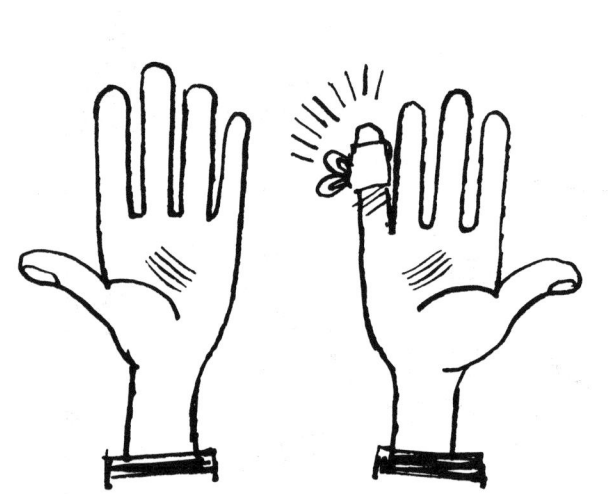

F (E*) One, two, **C (B7)** three, four, five, Once I caught a fish a-live;

C (B7) Six, se-ven, eight, nine, ten, **Bb(A)** **C (B7)** **F (E)** Then I let it go a-gain.

F (E) Why did you let it go? Be-cause it bit my **C (B7)** fin-ger so.

C (B7) Which fin-ger did it bite? **Bb(A)** **C (B7)** **F (E)** This lit-tle fin-ger on the right.

* capo on first fret may be used with alternative chords in brackets

35 Oranges and lemons

Oranges and lemons,
Say the bells of St Clement's.

You owe me five farthings,
Say the bells of St Martin's.

When will you pay me?
Say the bells of Old Bailey.

When I grow rich,
Say the bells of Shoreditch.

Pray, when will that be?
Say the bells of Stepney.

I do not know,
Says the great bell of Bow.

Old Father Baldpate,
Say the slow bells of Aldgate.

Pokers and tongs,
Say the bells of St John's.

Pancakes and fritters,
Say the bells of St Peter's.

Two sticks and an apple,
Say the bells of Whitechapel.

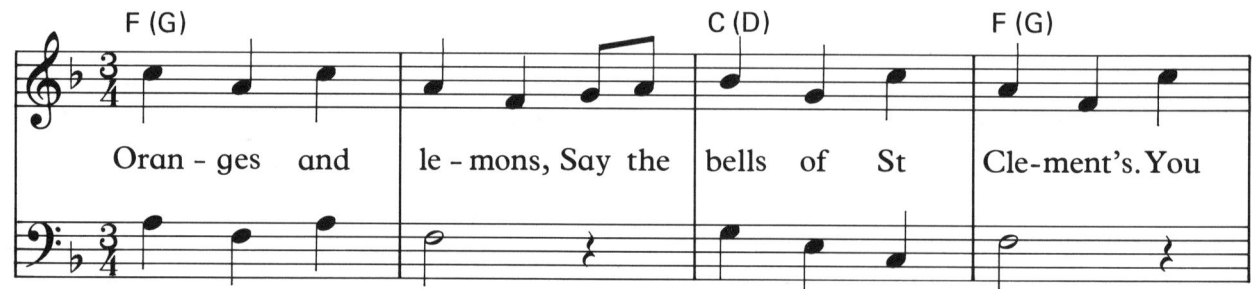

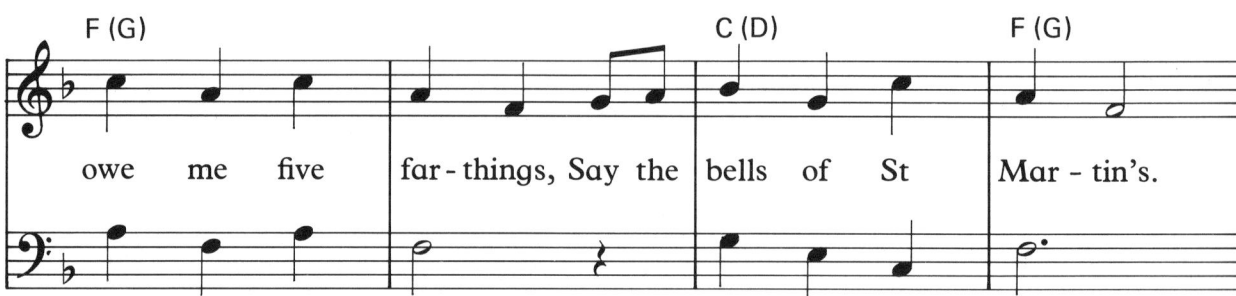

When I grow rich, Say the bells of Shore-ditch.

Here comes a can-dle to light you to bed, And

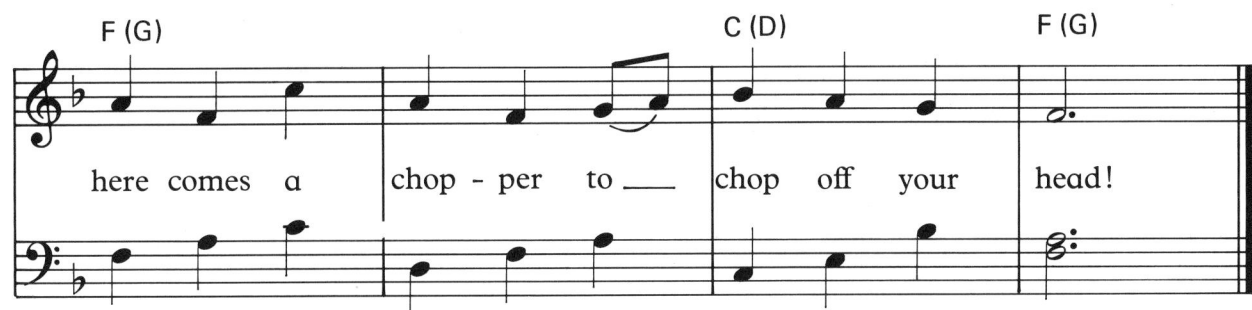

here comes a chop-per to chop off your head!

Kettles and pans,
Say the bells of St Anne's.

Brickbats and tiles,
Say the bells of St Giles'.

Here comes a candle
    to light you to bed,
And here comes a chopper
    to chop off your head!

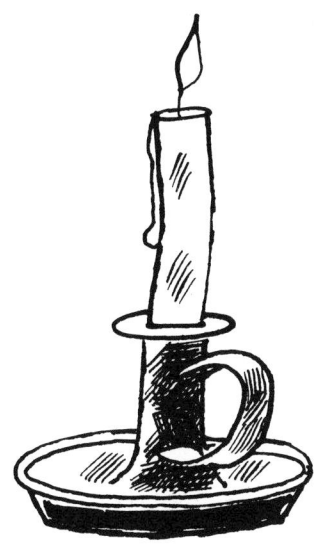

36 Pop goes the weasel

Half a pound of tuppenny rice,
Half a pound of treacle.
Mix it up and make it nice.
Pop goes the weasel!
Up and down the City Road,
In and out the Eagle,
That's the way the money goes.
Pop goes the weasel!

37 Here we go round the mulberry bush

Here we go round the mulberry bush,
The mulberry bush, the mulberry bush,
Here we go round the mulberry bush
On a cold and frosty morning.

This is the way we clap our hands,
Clap our hands, clap our hands,
This is the way we clap our hands
On a cold and frosty morning.

This is the way we stamp our feet,
Stamp our feet, stamp our feet,
This is the way we stamp our feet
On a cold and frosty morning.

This is the way we wash our clothes,
Wash our clothes, wash our clothes,
This is the way we wash our clothes
On a cold and frosty morning.

This is the way we iron our clothes,
Iron our clothes, iron our clothes,
This is the way we iron our clothes
On a cold and frosty morning.

This is the way we sweep the floor,
Sweep the floor, sweep the floor,
This is the way we sweep the floor
On a cold and frosty morning.

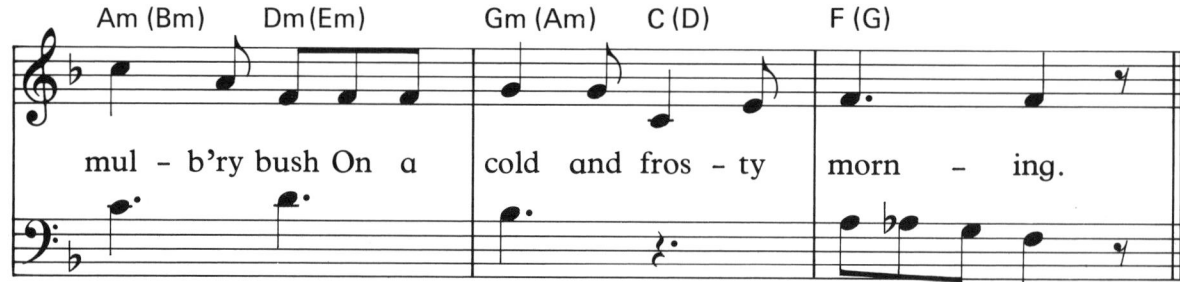

38 Ring-a-ring o' roses

Ring-a-ring o' roses,
A pocket full of posies.
A-tishoo! A-tishoo!
We'll all fall down.

The king has sent his daughter
To fetch a pail of water.
A-tishoo! A-tishoo!
We'll all fall down.

The bird upon the steeple
Sits high above the people.
A-tishoo! A-tishoo!
We'll all fall down.

The wedding bells are ringing,
The boys and girls are singing.
A-tishoo! A-tishoo!
We'll all fall down.

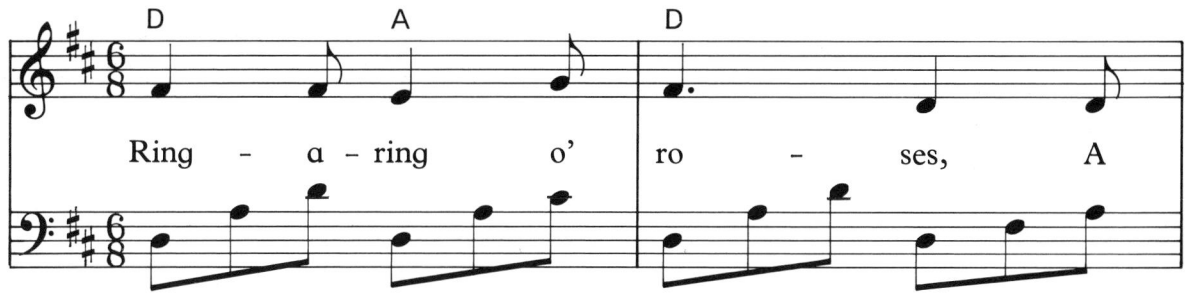

Ring - a - ring o' ro - ses, A

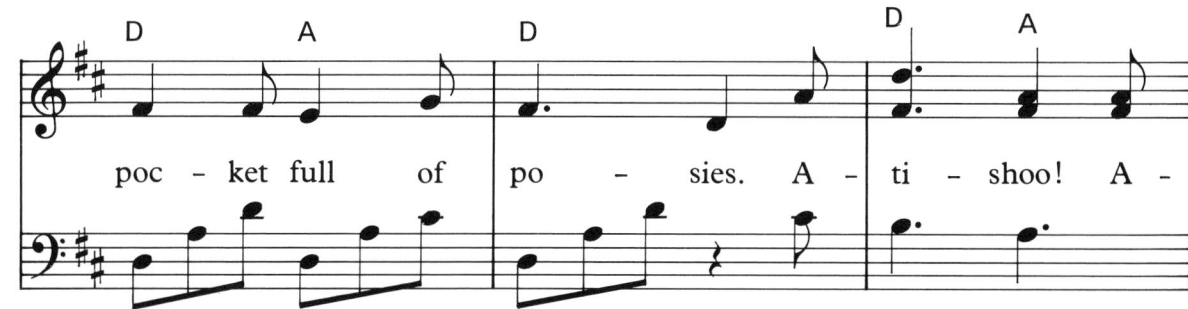

poc - ket full of po - sies. A - ti - shoo! A -

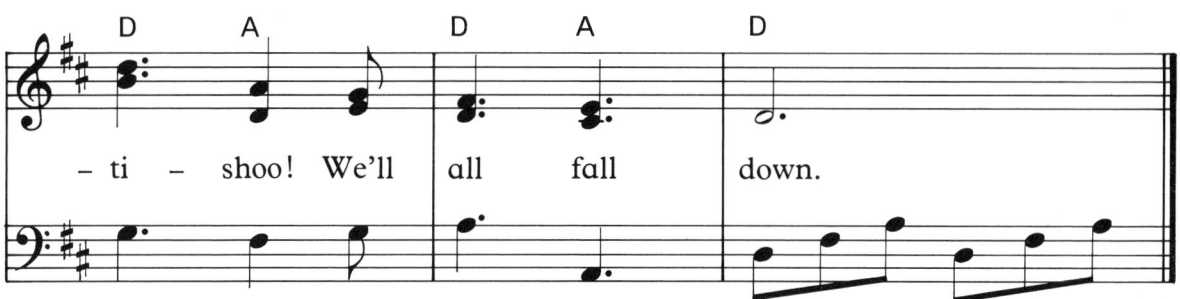

- ti - shoo! We'll all fall down.

39 There was a little girl

There was a little girl,
And she had a little curl,
Right in the middle of her forehead;
And when she was good,
She was very, very good,
But when she was bad,
She was horrid.

She stood upon her head
On her little truckle bed,
With nobody by for to hinder;
And she yelled and she yawled
And she screamed and she bawled,
And she banged her little heels
Against the window.

Her mother heard the noise,
And thought it was the boys
A-playing at a combat in the attic;
But when she climbed the stair,
And saw Jemima there,
She took and she did whip her
Most emphatic.

40 Old King Cole

Old King Cole was a merry old soul,
And a merry old soul was he;
He called for his pipe,
And he called for his bowl,
And he called for his fiddlers three.
Every fiddler had a fiddle fine,
And a very fine fiddle had he.
Oh, there's none so rare
As can compare
With King Cole and his fiddlers three.

Old King Cole was a merry old soul,
And a merry old soul was he;
He called for his pipe,
And he called for his bowl,
And he called for his pipers three.
Every piper had a pipe so fine,
And a very fine pipe had he.
Oh, there's none so rare
As can compare
With King Cole and his pipers three.

Old King Cole was a merry old soul,
And a merry old soul was he;
He called for his pipe,
And he called for his bowl,
And he called for his drummers three.
Every drummer had a drum so fine,
And a very fine drum had he.
Oh, there's none so rare
As can compare
With King Cole and his drummers three.

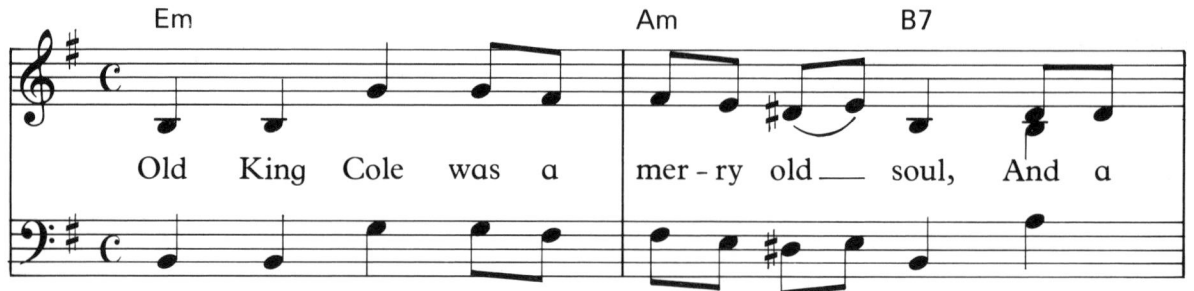

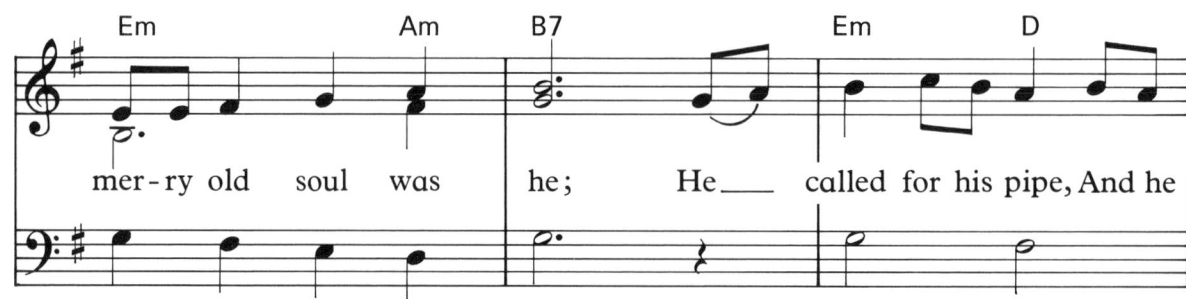

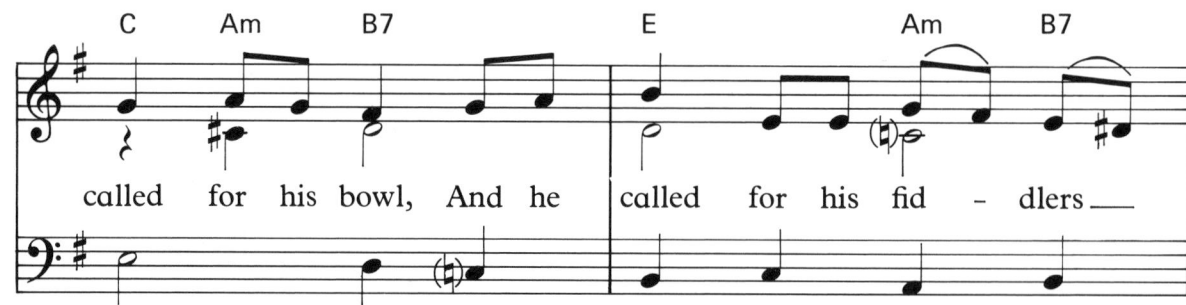

three. Ev – 'ry __ fid – dler __ had a fid-dle fine, And a

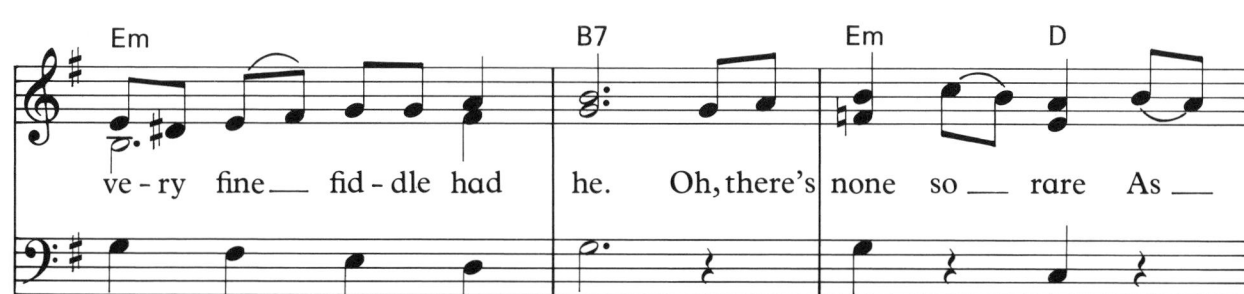

ve – ry fine __ fid-dle had he. Oh, there's none so __ rare As __

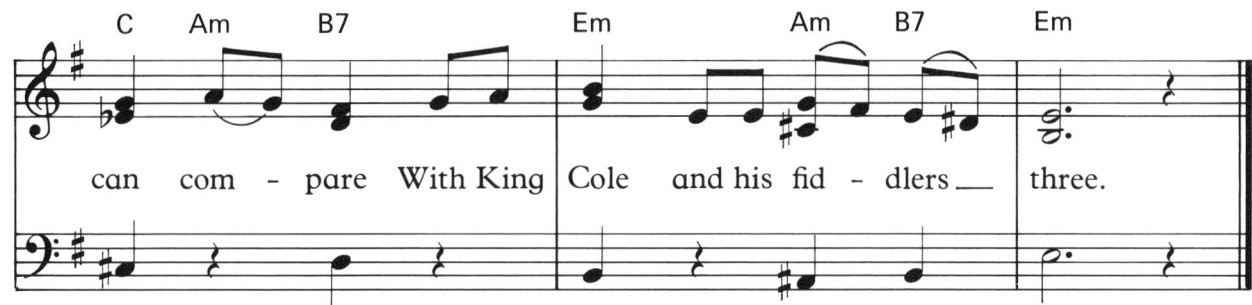

can com – pare With King Cole and his fid – dlers __ three.

41 Rub-a-dub-dub

Rub-a-dub-dub,
Three men in a tub,
And who do you think they be?
The butcher, the baker,
The candlestick-maker;
Turn 'em out! Knaves all three!

Rub - a - dub - dub, Three men in a tub, And

who do you think they be? _____ The

but - cher, the ba - ker, The can - dle - stick ma - ker;

Turn 'em out! Knaves all three!

42 Simple Simon

Simple Simon met a pieman
Going to the fair;
Said Simple Simon to the pieman,
"Let me taste your ware."

Said the pieman to Simple Simon,
"Show me first your penny;"
Said Simple Simon to the pieman,
"Sir, I have not any."

Simple Simon went a-fishing
For to catch a whale;
All the water he had got
Was in his mother's pail.

Simple Simon went to look
If plums grew on a thistle;
He pricked his fingers very much,
Which made poor Simon whistle.

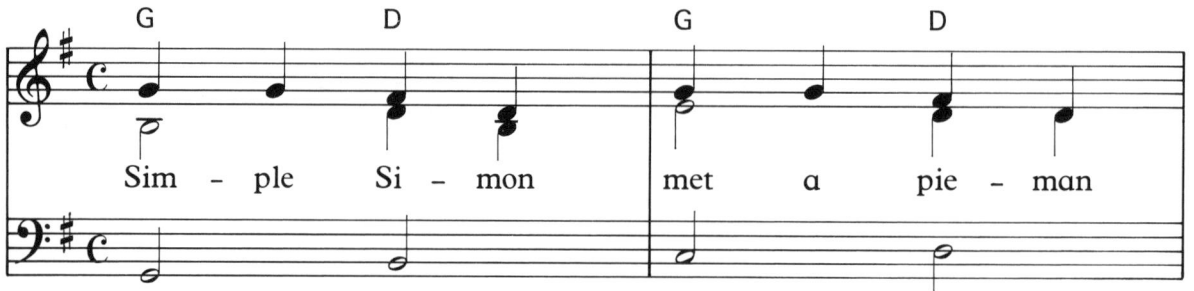

Sim - ple Si - mon   met   a   pie - man

Go - ing   to   the   fair;   Said   Sim - ple Si - mon

to   the pie - man,   "Let   me   taste   your   ware."

43 See-saw, Margery Daw

See-saw, Margery Daw,
Johnnie shall have a new master.
He shall earn but a penny a day,
Because he can't work any faster.

See-saw, sacaradown,
Which is the way to London town?
One foot up, the other foot down,
That is the way to London town.

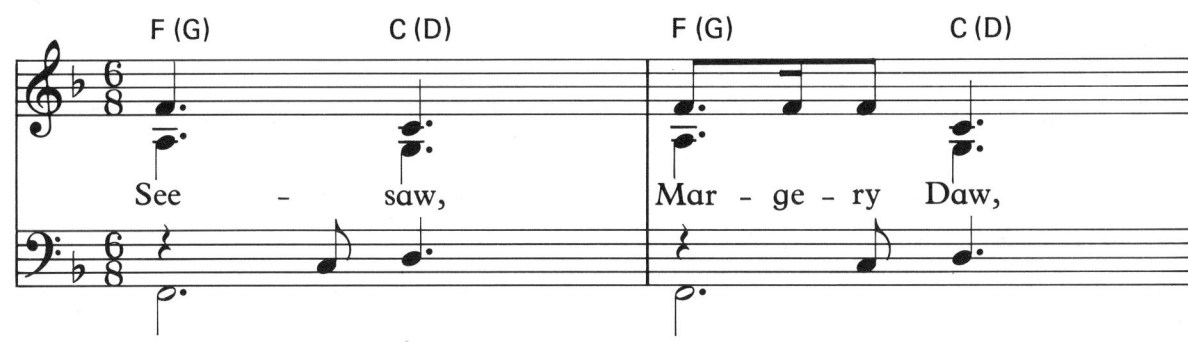

See - saw, Mar - ge - ry Daw,

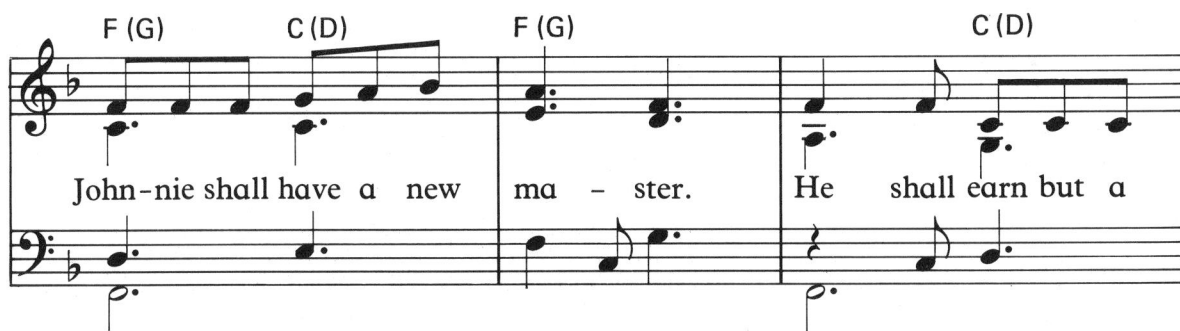

John - nie shall have a new ma - ster. He shall earn but a

pen - ny a day, Be - cause he can't work a - ny fa - ster.

44 Pat-a-cake

Pat-a-cake, pat-a-cake, baker's man,
Bake me a cake as fast as you can;
Pat it and prick it and mark it with B,
Put it in the oven for Baby and me.

Pat - a - cake, pat - a - cake, ba — ker's man,

Bake me a cake —— as fast as you can; Pat it and prick it and

mark it with B, Put it in the o - ven for Ba - by and me.

45 Old Mother Hubbard

Old Mother Hubbard,
She went to the cupboard,
To fetch her poor dog a bone;
But when she got there
The cupboard was bare,
And so the poor dog had none.

She took a clean dish
To get him some tripe,
But when she came back
He was smoking a pipe.

She went to the tailor's
To buy him a coat,
But when she came back
He was riding a goat.

She went to the hatter's
To buy him a hat,
But when she came back
He was feeding the cat.

She went to the barber's
To buy him a wig,
But when she came back
He was dancing a jig.

She went to the cobbler's
To buy him some shoes,
But when she came back
He was reading the news.

buy him a coat, But when she came back He was ri-ding a goat.

The dame made a curtsy,
The dog made a bow;
The dame said, "Your servant,"
The dog said, "Bow-wow."

46 Hey diddle diddle

Hey diddle diddle,
The cat and the fiddle,
The cow jumped over
   the moon.
The little dog laughed
To see such sport,
And the dish ran away
   with the spoon.

Hey did-dle did-dle, The cat and the fid-dle, The cow jumped o-ver the moon.____ The

lit-tle dog laughed To see such sport, And the dish ran a-way with the spoon.

* capo on first fret may be used with alternative chords in brackets

47 Jack Sprat

Jack Sprat could eat no fat,
His wife could eat no lean,
And so between them both, you see,
They licked the platter clean.

48 There was an old woman

There was an old woman tossed up in a basket,
Seventeen times as high as the moon;
Where she was going I couldn't but ask it,
For in her hand she carried a broom.
Old woman, old woman, old woman, quoth I,
O where are you going to, up so high?
To sweep the cobwebs out of the sky.
May I go with you?
Aye, by and by.

There was an old wo - man tossed up in a

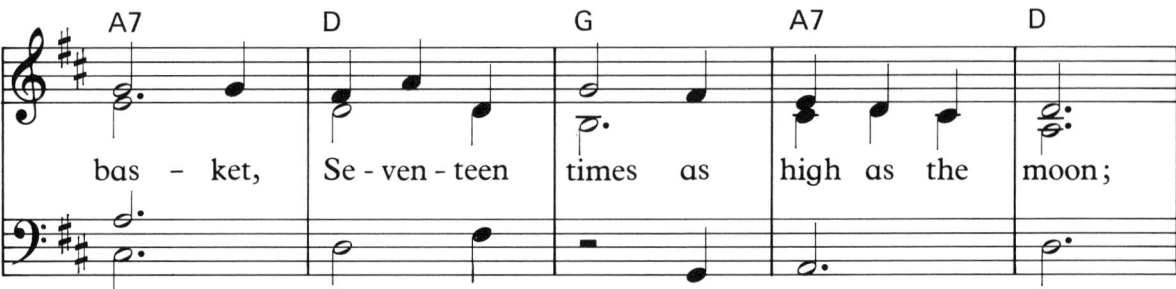

bas - ket, Se - ven - teen times as high as the moon;

Where she was go - ing I could - n't but ask it,

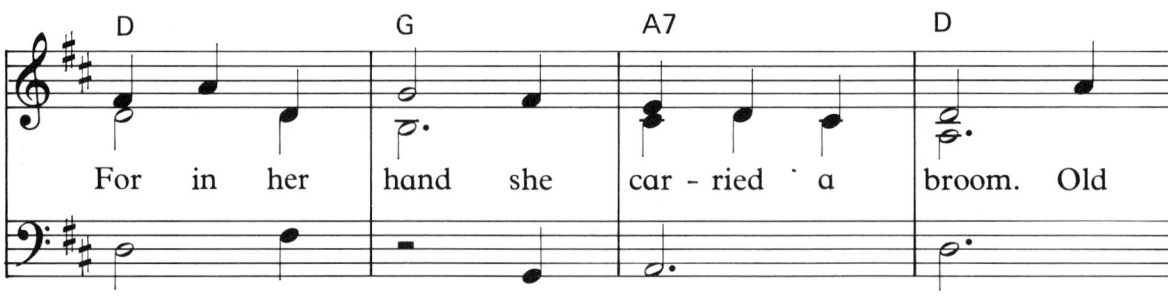

For in her hand she car - ried a broom. Old

49 Ride a cock-horse

Ride a cock-horse to Banbury Cross,
To see a fine lady upon a white horse;
Rings on her fingers and bells on her toes,
And she shall have music wherever she goes.

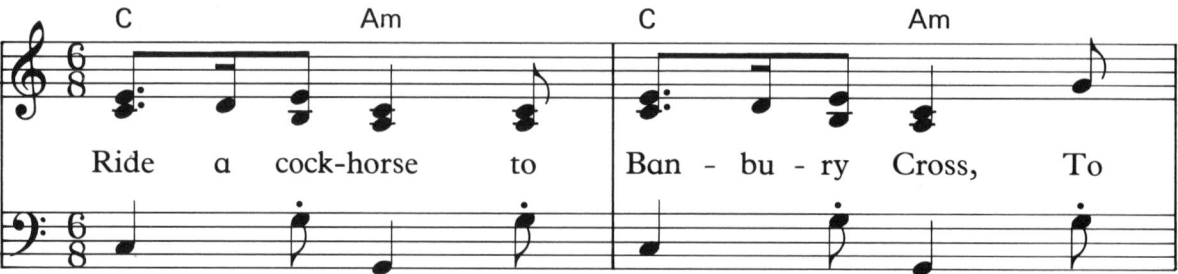

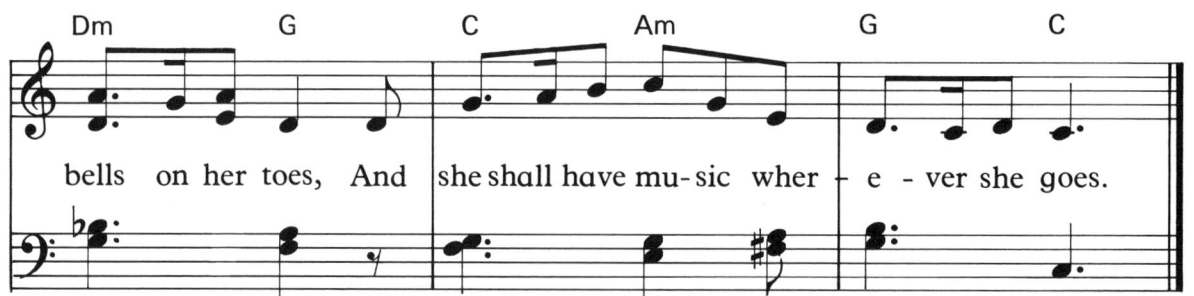

50 If all the world were paper

If all the world were paper,
And all the seas were ink,
And all the trees were bread and cheese,
What should we have to drink?
It's enough to make an old man
Scratch his head and think.

If all the world were pa - per, And all the seas were

ink, And all the trees were bread and cheese, What

should we have to drink? It's e - nough to make an

old man Scratch his head and think.

* capo on first fret may be used with alternative chords in brackets

51 What are little boys made of?

What are little boys made of?
What are little boys made of?
Frogs and snails and puppy-dogs' tails,
And such are little boys made of.

What are little girls made of?
What are little girls made of?
Sugar and spice and all things nice,
And such are little girls made of.

What are our young men made of?
What are our young men made of?
Sighs and leers and crocodile tears,
And such are our young men made of.

What are young women made of?
What are young women made of?
Ribbons and laces and sweet pretty faces,
And such are young women made of.

52 The grand old Duke of York

Oh, the grand old Duke of York,
He had ten thousand men;
He marched them up
   to the top of the hill
And he marched them down again.

And when they were up,
   they were up;
And when they were down,
   they were down;
And when they were only half way up,
They were neither up nor down.

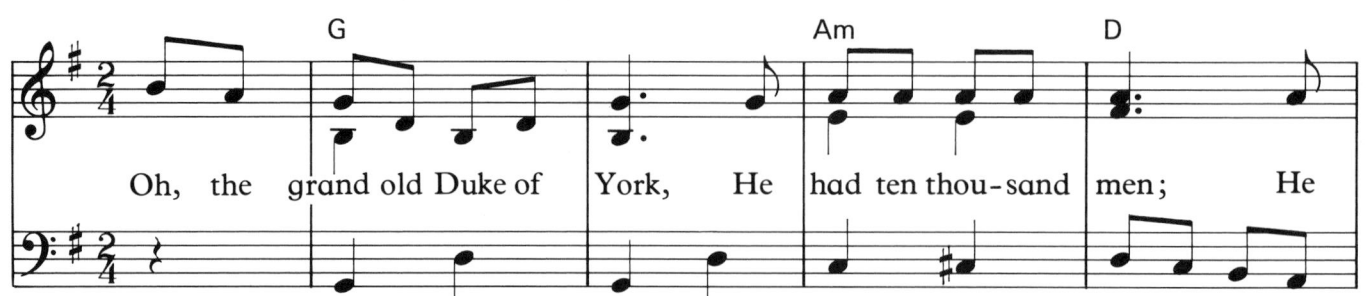

Oh, the grand old Duke of York, He had ten thou-sand men; He

marched them up to the top of the hill And he marched them down a - gain. And

when they were up, they were up; And when they were down, they were

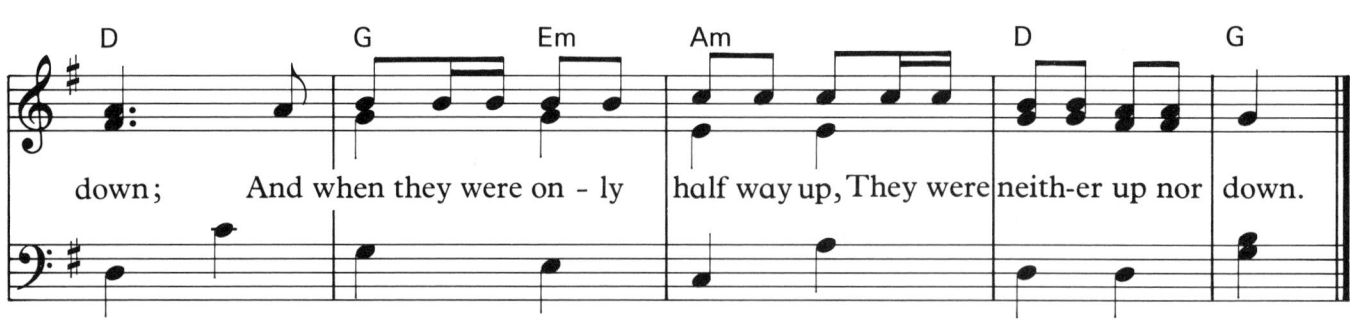

down; And when they were on - ly half way up, They were neith-er up nor down.

53 This old man

This old man, he played one,
He played nick nack on my drum.
Nick nack paddy whack, give a dog a bone,
This old man came rolling home.

This old man, he played two,
He played nick nack on my shoe . . .

This old man, he played three,
He played nick nack on the tree . . .

This old man, he played four,
He played nick nack on the door . . .

This old man, he played five,
He played nick nack on the hive . . .

This old man, he played six,
He played nick nack picking up sticks . . .

This old man, he played seven,
He played nick nack up to Heaven . . .

This old man, he played eight,
He played nick nack on the gate . . .

This old man, he played nine,
He played nick nack on a line . . .

This old man, he played ten,
He played nick nack with the hen . . .

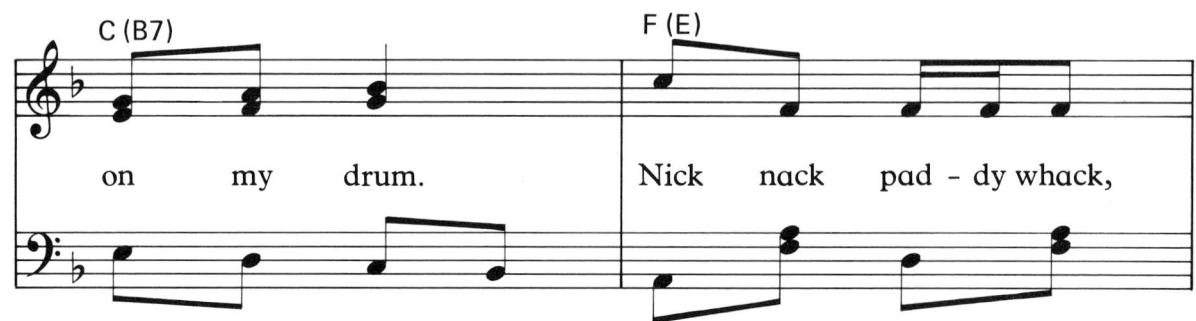

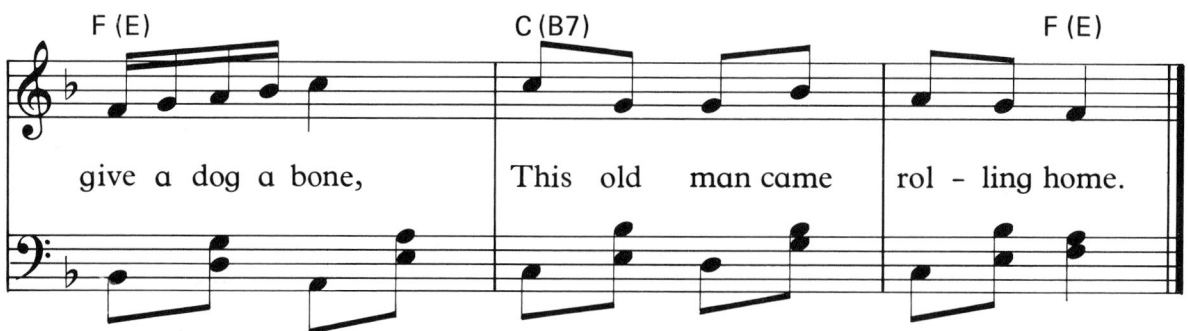

* capo on first fret may be used with alternative chords in brackets

54 Hark, hark, the dogs do bark

Hark, hark, the dogs do bark,
The beggars are coming to town;
Some in rags and some in jags
And some in velvet gown;
Some in rags and some in jags
And some in velvet gown.

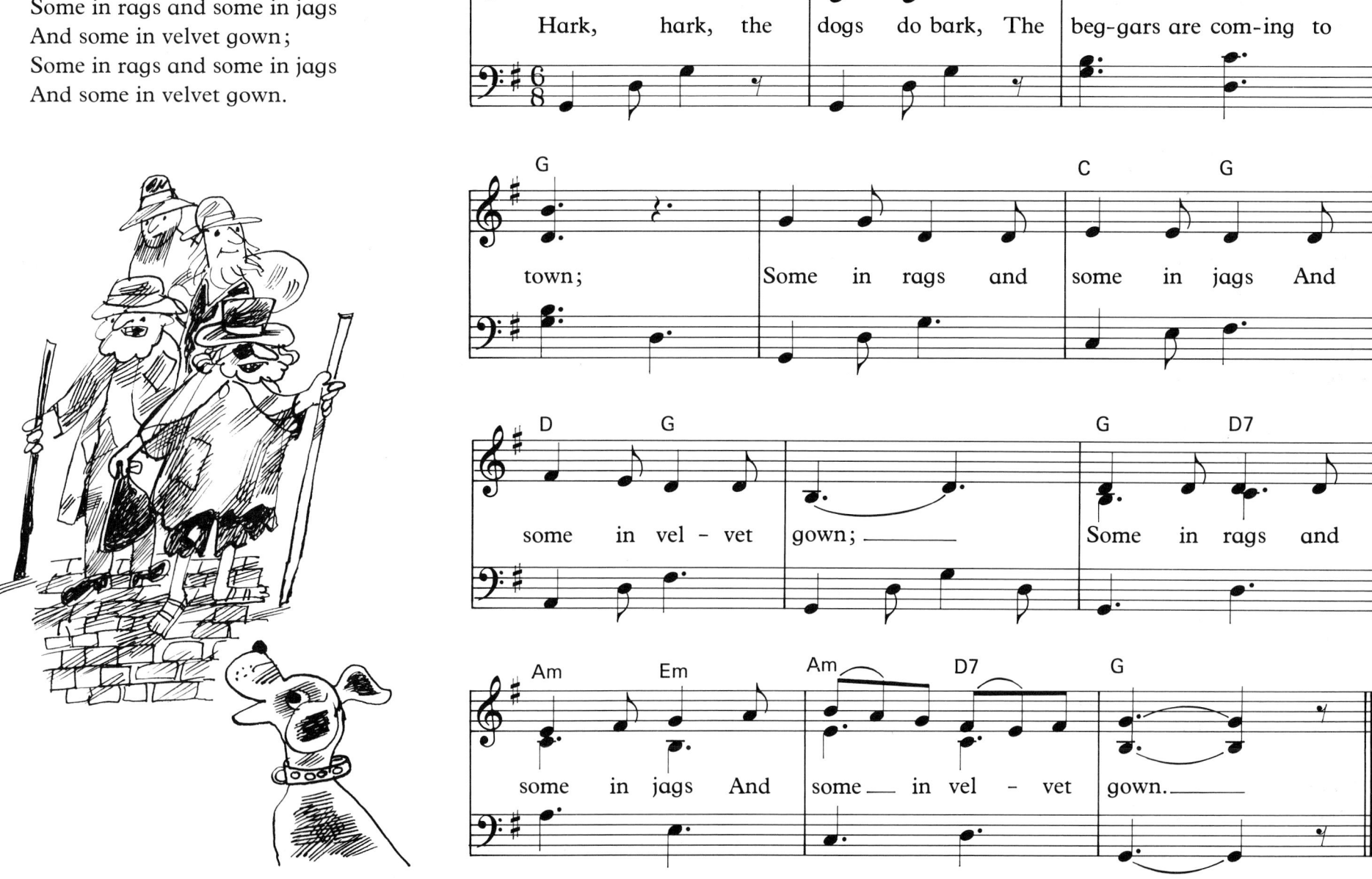

55 Curly locks

Curly locks, Curly locks,
  Will you be mine?
You shall not wash dishes,
  Nor yet feed the swine;
But sit on a cushion
  And sew a fine seam,
And feed upon strawberries,
  Sugar and cream.

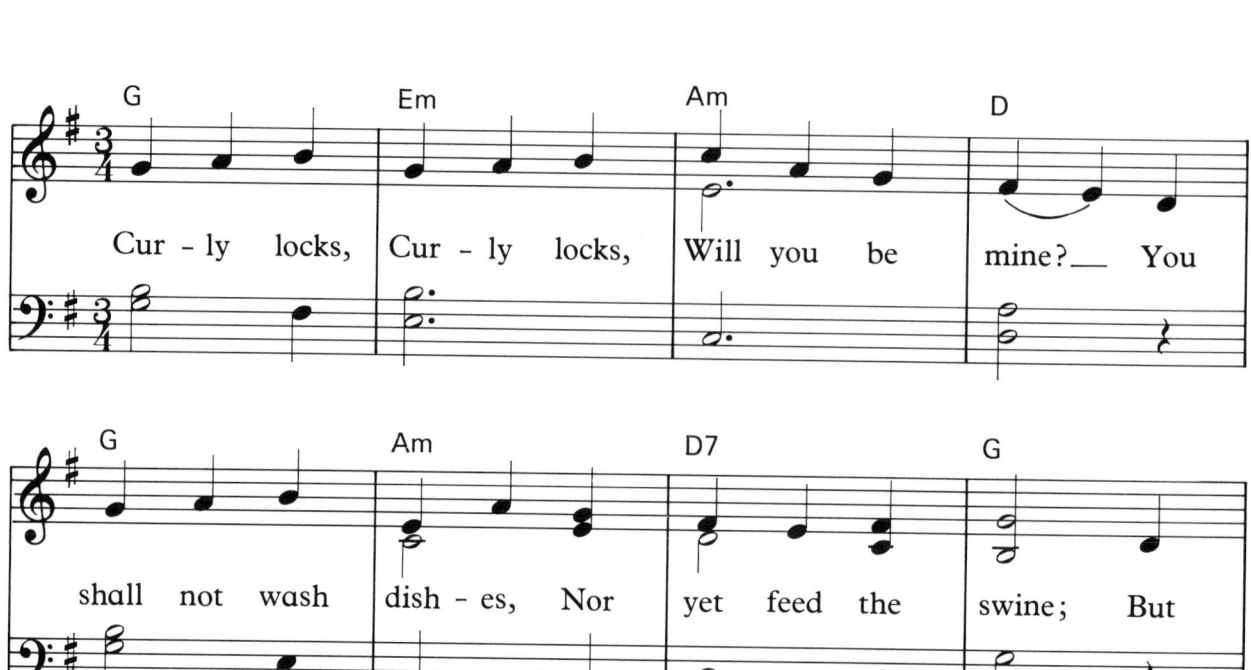

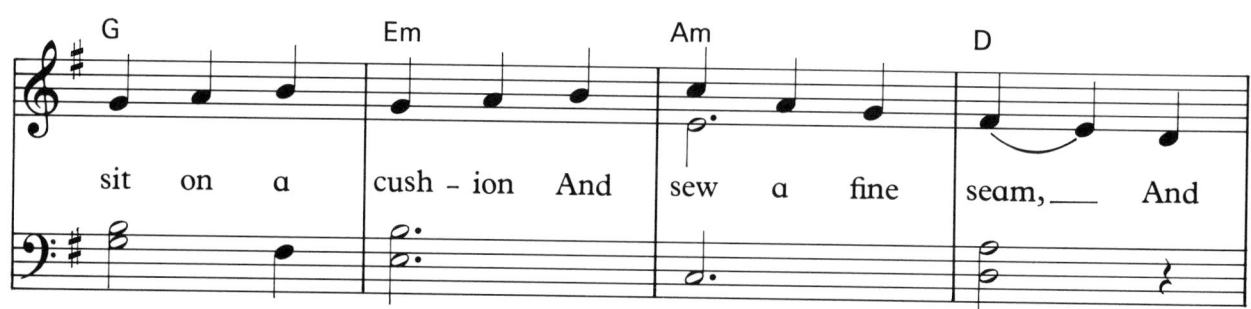

56 Yankee Doodle

Yankee Doodle came to town,
A-riding on a pony;
He stuck a feather in his cap
And called it macaroni.
    Yankee Doodle, keep it up,
    Yankee Doodle Dandy,
    Mind the music and the step,
    And with the girls be handy.

Marching in and marching out,
And marching round the town, O!
Here there comes a regiment
With Captain Thomas Brown, O!
    Yankee Doodle, keep it up . . .

Yankee Doodle is a tune
That comes in mighty handy;
The enemy all runs away
At Yankee Doodle Dandy.
    Yankee Doodle, keep it up . . .

57 Hickory, dickory, dock

Hickory, dickory, dock,
The mouse ran up the clock.
The clock struck one, the mouse ran down,
Hickory, dickory, dock.

Hickory, dickory, dare,
The pig flew up in the air.
The man in brown soon brought him down,
Hickory, dickory, dare.

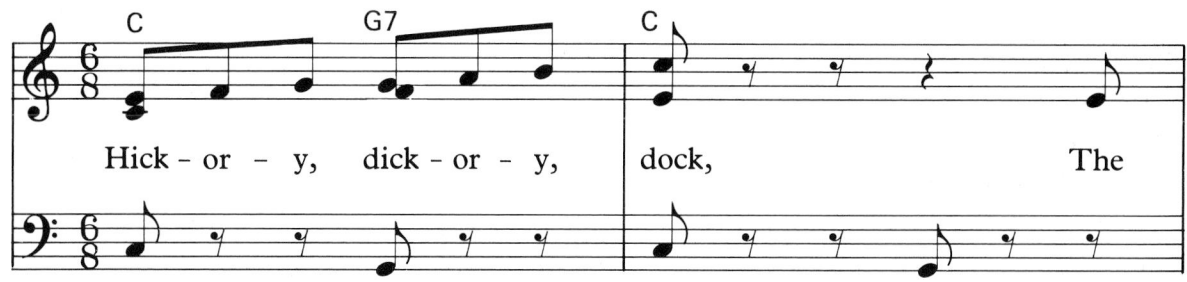

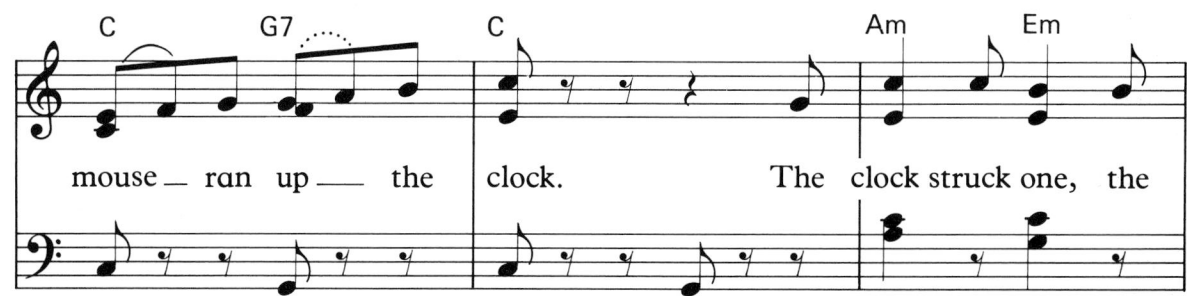

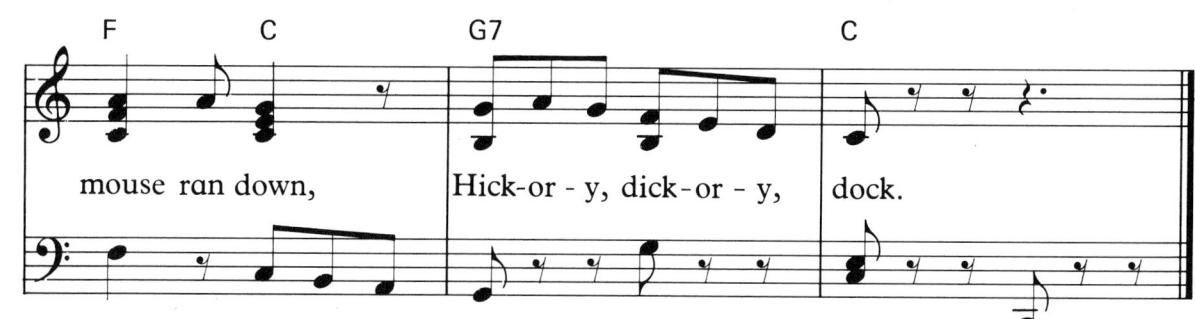

58 Little Polly Flinders

Little Polly Flinders
Sat among the cinders,
Warming her pretty little toes;
Her mother came and caught her,
And whipped her little daughter
For spoiling her nice new clothes.

59 Polly, put the kettle on

Polly, put the kettle on,
Polly, put the kettle on,
Polly, put the kettle on,
We'll all have tea.

Sukey, take it off again,
Sukey, take it off again,
Sukey, take it off again,
They've all gone away.

Pol-ly, put the ket-tle on, Pol-ly, put the ket-tle on,

Pol-ly, put the ket-tle on, We'll all have tea.

Su-key, take it off a-gain, Su-key, take it off a-gain,

Su-key, take it off a-gain, They've all gone a-way.

* capo on first fret may be used with alternative chords in brackets

60 Good King Arthur

When good King Arthur ruled this land,
  He was a goodly king;
He stole three pecks of barley meal
  To make a bag-pudding.

A bag-pudding the king did make,
  And stuffed it well with plums;
And in it put great lumps of fat,
  As big as my two thumbs.

The king and queen did eat thereof,
  And noblemen beside;
And what they could not eat that night,
  The queen next morning fried.

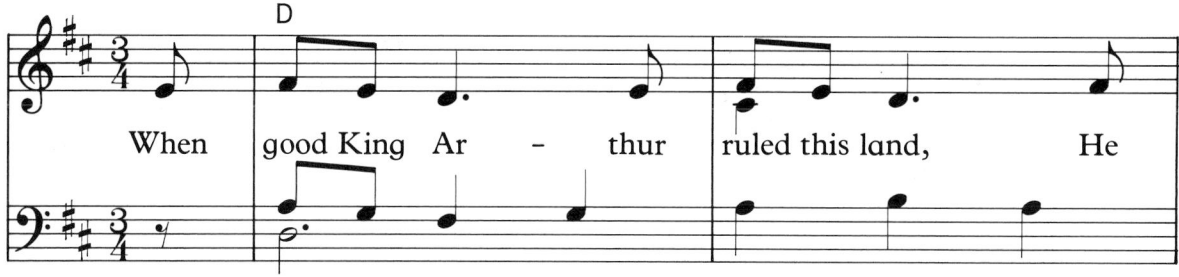

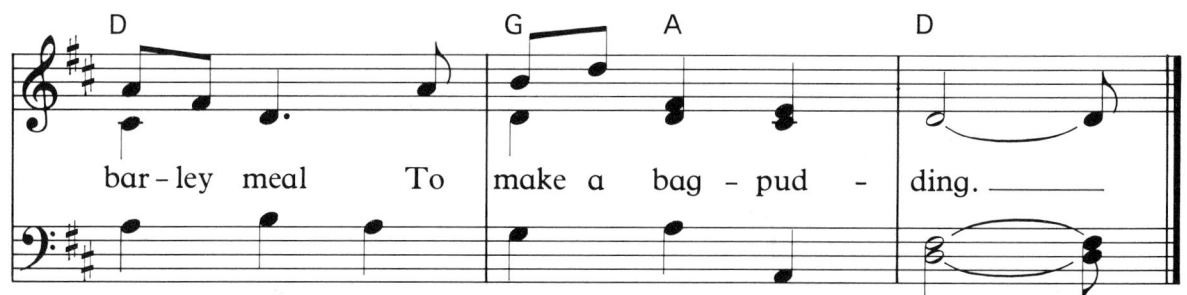

61 I had a little nut tree

I had a little nut tree,
   Nothing would it bear
But a silver nutmeg
   And a golden pear;
The King of Spain's daughter
   Came to visit me,
And all for the sake of
   My little nut tree.

62 Hot cross buns

Hot cross buns,
Hot cross buns,
One a penny, two a penny,
Hot cross buns.
If you have no daughters,
Give them to your sons,
One a penny, two a penny,
Hot cross buns.

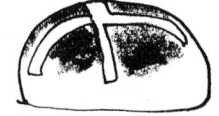

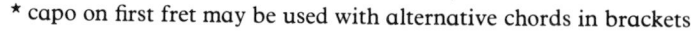

* capo on first fret may be used with alternative chords in brackets

63 Dame, get up and bake your pies

Dame, get up and bake your pies,
Bake your pies, bake your pies,
Dame, get up and bake your pies
On Christmas Day in the morning.

Dame, what makes your maidens lie,
Maidens lie, maidens lie?
Dame, what makes your maidens lie
On Christmas Day in the morning?

Dame, what makes your ducks to die,
Ducks to die, ducks to die?
Dame, what makes your ducks to die
On Christmas Day in the morning?

Their wings are cut, they cannot fly,
Cannot fly, cannot fly,
Their wings are cut, they cannot fly,
On Christmas Day in the morning.

Dame, get up and bake your pies,

Bake your pies, bake your pies,

Dame, get up and bake your pies On

Christ - mas Day in the morn - ing.

64 Upon Paul's steeple

Upon Paul's steeple stands a tree
As full of apples as may be;
The little boys of London town
They run with hooks to pull them down;
And then they run from hedge to hedge
Until they come to London Bridge.

N.B. The left hand has the tune.
The right hand plays one octave higher than written.

65 Twinkle, twinkle, little star

Twinkle, twinkle, little star,
How I wonder what you are,
Up above the world so high,
Like a diamond in the sky.
    Twinkle, twinkle, little star,
    How I wonder what you are.

When the blazing sun is gone,
When he nothing shines upon,
Then you show your little light,
Twinkle, twinkle, all the night.

Then the traveller in the dark
Thanks you for your tiny spark;
Could he see which way to go
If you did not twinkle so?

In the dark blue sky you keep,
While you through my curtains peep,
And you never shut your eye
Till the sun is in the sky.

66 Wee Willie Winkie

Wee Willie Winkie
  Runs through the town,
Upstairs and downstairs
  In his night-gown,
Rapping at the window,
  Crying through the lock,
"Are the children all in bed,
  For now it's eight o'clock?"

Wee — Wil - lie Win - kie Runs through the town,

Up - stairs and down - stairs In his night gown,

Rap-ping at the win - dow, Cry-ing through the lock, "Are the

chil - dren all in bed, For now it's eight o' - clock?"

Guitar chords

Guitar chords are provided for all the songs except 64 "Upon Paul's steeple". Some songs have easier alternative chords in brackets.
When using these alternative chords, the placing of a capo on first fret will allow the following songs to be sung in the same key as written: songs 1, 5, 6, 9, 14, 23, 26, 28, 34, 46, 50, 53, 59, 62.

Here are all the guitar chords in this book. A cross above a string means that it should not be sounded.
A bracket linking two or more strings indicates that they should be held down simultaneously by the first finger.

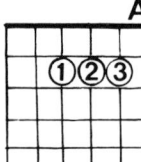

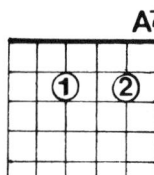

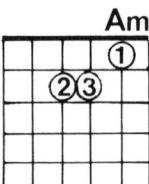

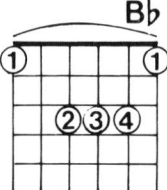

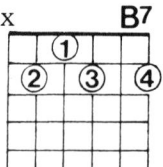

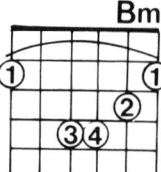

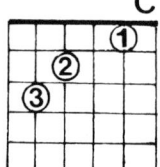

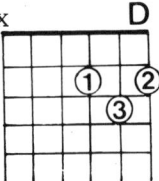

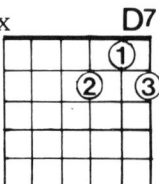

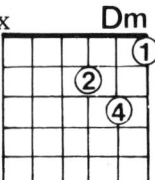

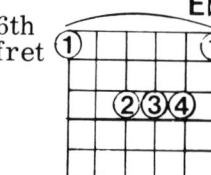

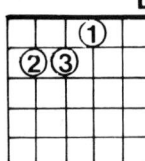

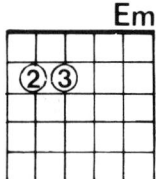

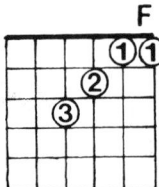

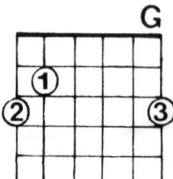

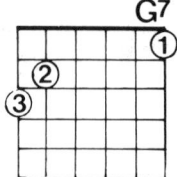

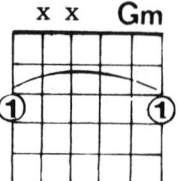